AROUND THE TENTS OF TORAH

AROUND THE TENTS OF TORAH

COMMENTARY ON THE BIBLE

Rabbi N. L. Marcus

AMBERLEY

First published 1973
This edition published 2022

Amberley Publishing
The Hill, Stroud
Gloucestershire, GL5 4EP

www.amberley-books.com

Copyright © N. L. Marcus, 1973

The right of N. L. Marcus to be identified as the Author
of this work has been asserted in accordance with the
Copyrights, Designs and Patents Act 1988.

All rights reserved. No part of this book may be reprinted
or reproduced or utilised in any form or by any electronic,
mechanical or other means, now known or hereafter invented,
including photocopying and recording, or in any information
storage or retrieval system, without the permission in writing
from the Publishers.

British Library Cataloguing in Publication Data.
A catalogue record for this book is available from the British Library.

ISBN 978 1 3981 0448 8 (paperback)

Typeset in 10pt on 12pt Sabon.
Typesetting and Origination by Amberley Publishing.
Printed in the UK.

TRANSLATION OF LETTER WRITTEN BY RABBI CH. L. SHMUELOWITZ DEAN OF MIR YESHIVA

I have seen parts of the work of my friend, the esteemed and widely known Rabbi Nachurn Leib Marcus, minister of the Vredehoek Hebrew Congregation, Cape Town, dealing with the parshiyot of the Torah. They contain worthy ideas expressed in a sincere and God-fearing spirit and bound to be attractive to all readers.

I have known my friend since his student days in the Yeshiva of Mir in Europe when he was already a scholar of note; latterly I have also heard of his devoted labours to strengthen Judaism and Torah in his city, and I send him my blessing and hope that his creative endeavours will continue undiminished so that his endeavours to spread and deepen Torah-knowledge and our faith will be crowned with success in his country of abode.

CHAIM SHMUELOWITZ

ב"ה ולמנחם יג"א

הופיעו לפני קונטרסים מחודדו"ח ונדיבו להכתב
(כעניינים שונים תמוזות) את אלהדר בתוב לנו אוהבינו שליט"א
כף הקהלות לישיבות הק' ישי"ע אתמודי בפני הבית י"להמי"ד
4 סדר קראות התורה והדף קוועית למציבי ה'מלאצינים
אמונך ולהם ש הונה לעבדם לקו מעלים, ונפש מה יד אות
ויהי רצון מלפני ... איד אמונים לעודד ... הוישמו של
ישיבת מיר כחול, ולפי דלג"ק הקאינו להצילו והפאלת גזירת
לישמש מעליוצא בעומדו לחינוף להמנה נפוהב...
כתני', והנה והדל כי יקבלו מעינות מוצא
וינה לעולם קן הסעבה לה'תור רבדינו הלגדל
לעב ולהנהות.
(בחתם ומעל) ושב בעמם

שמ'ל שמואלוביץ

FOREWORD

There is a considerable lack of good sermon material in English, and the present work represents an excellent contribution towards making good this desideratum.

An interesting feature of this book is that it is not so much concerned with direct moralising and exhortation as it is with conveying, in readable form, a wealth of homiletic material based upon ancient Midrashim and other classical sources not otherwise readily available to the English reader. From this point of view the volume will fulfil an important educational need.

The author, Rabbi Marcus of Cape Town, is well equipped for the compilation of such a work. Steeped in the learning of the fine old Yeshiva tradition, he is at the same time open to the ways of the present day western world; and his religious fervour and sincerity are everywhere apparent.

I have great pleasure in commending this work. It will undoubtedly enhance the sacred values of our People in an age that is increasingly looking for guidance and inspiration.

C. B. Casper,
Chief Rabbi
1973

PREFACE

Every child has a name, equally every book is given a name. In most instances the naming of a child is associated with family events. Many a book has its origin (and root) in the past of its author. From my early childhood, I was fortunate in being directly connected with the "Tents of Torah".

The house where I was brought up in Mir was not far from the famous Mirer Yeshiva. The lyrical sounds, songs and tunes which the Yeshiva Bachurim sang while they meditated and grappled with Talmudical problems, penetrated into the precincts of our house. At the age of thirteen I was already accepted into the above Yeshiva. I was already able to understand a "Blat-Gemorah", without the help of a Talmud teacher. In time I obtained my smicha from the late Gaon Eliezer-Yehudah Finkel, of blessed memory, the Dean of the Mirer Yeshivah.

My late parents encouraged me to study and love Talmud and did not spare themselves in order to enable me to pursue my studies.

Shortly after my arrival in this country, I was fortunate enough to be associated with the Beth-Hamedrash Hechadash in Cape Town where a daily Talmud Shiur had already been in existence for many years. So here once again I remained near to the "Tents of Torah".

Rabbi N. L. Marcus

This has prompted me to name my book "Around the Tents of Torah". I do not propose to delve to the great depths of our Torah; what I merely desire to do is to focus light on some aspect or other of the area "Around the Tents of the Torah".

I wish to express my deepest and profound appreciation to the following people:

To Mr. M. E. Katz, principal of Herzlia school, for his sincere and friendly advice; to Mr. L. Leiserovitz and Mr. J. Geffin for their financial help.

In great humility I thank the Almighty for granting me strength to study Torah.

N. L. Marcus

GENESIS

Genesis: "In the beginning the Lord created heaven and earth."

Midrash: Rav Huna said in the name of Rav Matna: "The Lord created the world because of the following three objects which are also called 'beginnings', which the People of Israel will give to the Priests: chalah (the first dough), ma'aser (the tithe), and bikkurum (the first fruits).

The above statement by Rav Huna contains a deep thought. It was the duty of the farmer to give a portion of his harvest to the priests. But then the farmer may object and ask: "Why should I part with a portion of my wealth for which I toiled to give to people who have done nothing for the cultivation of the land?" The Torah, therefore, admonishes the farmer not to forget that everything was granted to him by the grace of the Lord. The rains have fallen in time, there were no storms and mildew. Everything was orderly and this was largely due to the prayers and supplications which were rendered in the Holy Temple. "Do not think, farmer, that it was by your own strength and effort that you were able to accumulate your fortune. It is your duty to appreciate what the Lord has done for you, and thank the Lord by practical and charitable deeds, by supporting and helping the poor and needy."

The wars, conflicts and revolutions of history are rooted in greed and arrogance.

Our conception is different; every human being has to acknowledge and to remember that the Lord has created the world, thus the honour and greatness belong to Him. If that thought would have been accepted by all the nations, then peace and brotherhood would have prevailed among all people. In a similar way our Sages have interpreted the verse, "and it was evening", as referring to Esau, implying that as Esau does not believe in the

Lord, therefore he is the cause of darkness, bloodshed, murder and plunder in the world.

"And it was morning", according to this interpretation, refers to Jacob, who by his belief in the Lord brings light and tranquillity to mankind.

Rabbi Yitzchak said: "The Torah ought to have started with the commandment of Exodus 122: "This month belongs to you," as this is the first commandment in the Bible. Why then is it that the Bible starts with the creation of the world? The answer is that the Lord has already decided to give the land to the People of Israel, thus anticipating the accusation of the nations who might come later and complain that the People of Israel were robbers who had taken possession of a land which did not belong to them. He accordingly provided the answer: "I created the world, thus I possess the right of distribution to whom I choose." Rabbi Yitzchak was living at a sad period for our People. We were oppressed and downtrodden and always the scapegoat of evil-minded persons. Eretz-Israel was occupied by other nations. Although we never gave up hope of redemption, its realisation seemed beyond possibility. The Rabbi understood the mood of the people, their disappointments and grief, so he comforted them and pointed out the fact that the Lord had created the world and for Him there is nothing impossible to achieve and to give.

Accordingly we find that the theme of the land of Israel bound up with the People of Israel permeates the Bible. Abraham was promised the land (Genesis: 13-17): "Get up walk in the land. Arise walk through the land in the length of it and in the breadth of it for unto thee will I give it." Then Abraham asked the Lord (15-8): "O, Lord, whereby shall I know that I shall inherit it?" That question seems at first glance difficult to understand. Abraham, the great believer in the Lord, wavered in his faith? He, who was tested by the Lord ten times and withstood all the tests, should suddenly lose faith in the promise of the Lord?

He certainly remained in his strong belief, but his question concerned his children. He asked whether his children would be willing to leave behind them their comfortable and luxurious homes in the Galut and settle in Israel which would have to be cultivated and developed by hard work and superhuman exertion. Would they agree to exchange their peaceful and spacious homes for the turbulent and dangerous dwellings in Israel? To that pertinent question the Lord provided an answer (13) when He said to Abraham: "Know of surety that thy seed shall be a stranger in a land that is not theirs and shall serve them and they shall afflict them 400 years." The affliction, oppression and pogroms in the diaspora would eventually force them to seek and strive for their land.

The prophet Isaiah has foreseen it in his prophecy (6-8): "Who are these that fly as a cloud and as the doves to their cotes?" The flying of a cloud is forced, it is driven by the wind, whereas the flying of doves is a voluntary action. They are coming to their nests with love and cheerfulness. The prophet foresees that some of us will be driven by force to the land like a cloud. We shall have no choice in the matter, whereas some of our brethren will be returning like children after a long absence, into the outstretched arms of their waiting parents. That is one concept of the Mother Land. Israel will receive them as a mother embraces her beloved children who return home.

Isaac also received a promise from the Lord (Gen. 26-3): "So journey in this land and I will be with thee for unto thee and unto thy seed I will give all those lands." Isaac was more fortunate in this respect. Whereas the other Patriarchs had to wander away from the land of Israel, Isaac never left the land from his birth until his death.

Jacob was equally promised (Gen. 28-13): "The land on which thou liest, to thee will I give it and to thy seed."

It may be explained that the above three promises correspond to the three times that we entered the land. The first time we entered under the leadership of Joshua. The conquest was not so difficult. That entrance into the land corresponds to the promise which the Lord gave to Abraham: "Get up, walk in the land."

The second time we came into the land was under the leadership of Ezra. We were encouraged to go to Israel by Cyrus of Persia. Hence there was no fighting and strife while taking possession of the land, which indeed corresponds to the promise made to Isaac: "So journey in this land."

The third entry was a different matter. We had to battle for every inch of the soil. Innumerable sacrifices were brought on the altar of our land. This reflects the words which the Lord said to Jacob: "The land which thou liest to thee I give it." Namely, you have to lie on the land, not to move an inch, in spite of the difficulties. You have to remain steadfast. It is our national anchor which prevents us from drifting away in the currents of life.

In the creation of Adam the Lord said: "Let us make a man." The Midrash comments that among the Angels there was an argument whether Adam should be created The representative of truth objected, giving the reason that man is false and tells lies. Then Gemilut-chesed (charity), intervened and supported the creation of man, as he is charitable and helps the poor. Peace voted against, saying that man is warlike and quarrelsome. But Zedaka supported it, saying that man is sometimes kind. It was a stalemate, two against two. What did the Lord do? He took truth and threw it down and thus the Lord obtained a majority and Adam was created.

There is a difficult question: Why did the Lord drop down Truth in order to obtain a majority? He could have dropped

Peace and the same majority could have been obtained. To that question there is a logical answer. Had Truth remained in heaven, then Adam would not have been created, as there is no majority against Truth, as there is one truth only which is not ruled by majorities. As our faith is presently in a minority and yet we do not accept the faith of the majorities, because we believe that our faith constitutes the Truth.

NOAH

Opinions among the Rabbis vary as to whether Noah was really a worthy and holy person. Some maintain that Noah was considered to be worthy only if contrasted with his wicked and sinful contemporaries, but had he lived in a more pious generation, he would have been accepted as an ordinary person. This opinion may be corroborated from the text of the Bible (6-9): "With the Lord walked Noah," implying that he was like a small child who had to be guided and led carefully by the hand.

Noah, it seems, was helpless and powerless to influence and change the wicked people. So the Lord told him to build an ark, where he could live according to his convictions, without any outside interference. Maimonides has expressed a similar idea. When a pious person comes to a place where religion is abused and degraded, he should, according to Maimonides, segregate himself and lead a lonely life. When it is impossible for the righteous to impress and change the sinners, then the best way out of that dilemma is to retire as it were to oneself. The prophet Elijah found himself in the same situation. He tried his utmost to win over the sinful King Ahab to his side, but his exertions ended in complete failure, as Ahab returned to his former idol-worship. Elijah asked the Lord to take his soul, because he had considered his mission accomplished in this world and there was nothing more for him to do. The Lord would not do so, however, as the time of the prophet's natural death had not arrived yet. So the Lord granted him a compromise in that he went up alive to heaven.

The Lord instructed Noah about the dimensions and construction of the ark, including the making of a window. The Midrash comments: "There was a pearl hanging on the ceiling, which illuminated the whole ark and gave ample light to all who were inside it." It was already remarked by our Rabbis that while Noah was in the ark, there was peace and unity among all those present in the vessel, but as soon as they left the ark, arguments and wars started among the children and the descendants of Noah. While they were in the ark, the pearl – the riches and wealth – was accessible to all alike. There were no class differences between haves and have-nots. It gave light to all the people without any distinction of race and creed. But as soon as they left the ark, differences and distinctions were created, leading to strife, struggle and wars.

(8-8) "And he sent forth a dove from him to see if the waters were abated from the face of the ground. But the dove found no rest for the sole of her foot and she returned unto him to the ark for the waters were on the face of the earth."

The Yalkut refers (5a) to the verse (Deut. 21): "and among those nations you will not find a rest." This may be explained as follows: The people of Israel were compared to a dove by King Solomon in "The Song of Songs." Ever since the dove has remained the symbol and sign of peace and tranquillity. During our long history of suffering we have tried to live in peace and harmony with all the peoples of the world, but unfortunately, the world has rejected and humiliated us. With the help of the

Lord, we have succeeded throughout the ages in retaining our identity. But after the Ghetto walls began to crumble and many of our People were emancipated; they left their nation entirely and became assimilated. Like the dove who left the ark never to return again.

Our Rabbis (M'Gila) tell us that King Ahasuerus made a feast and invited all the Jewish subjects to it. Although the food was not Kosher, it did not stop them from participating and enjoying the party. But no sooner had Hamman appeared on the scene, with his cruel and menacing decrees, then the Hebrews returned to Judaism. Similarly with the dove. She left the ark with the intention of abandoning her peaceful place. But when she failed to secure a resting place for the sole of her feet, she returned home. It was as if the outside world did not accept her; she felt excluded from society. The analogy is obvious.

"And the dove came in to him at eventide and in her mouth an olive-leaf freshly plucked." The Rabbis comment thus: the olive-leaf she brought from Israel.

The following analogy may be considered: Whenever there is natural calamity, be it flood or fire the first to suffer and to be blamed are the People of Israel. In Gitin (55), we have the story of the Roman General sent by the Romans to destroy Israel. At first he was reluctant to fulfil his mission, so he shot an arrow into the sky that it should indicate the direction to be followed by his army. Subsequently, whichever side he shot, the arrow fell in the direction of Israel. The implication is that whatever calamity occurs in the world, the Jews are blamed. We are invariably blamed for all the wars, revolutions and upheavals wherever they may occur. The only place of peace and safety is in Israel.

After the flood, the Lord made a covenant (9-13): "I have set My rainbow in the cloud and it shall be for you a token of a Covenant between Me and the earth and it shall come to pass, when I bring clouds over the earth and the rainbow is seen, that I will remember My Covenant." The rainbow consists of many colours, and yet one colour does not obliterate or swallow up the others. They exist side by side in peace and harmony. There is enough room for everybody to live and prosper. This indicates the pattern and situation of humanity in the future, namely, that nations and peoples can live and exist together in mutual understanding and peace. So long as there is no desire to dominate or subjugate, the prophecy of Isaiah, that the lamb will dwell in peace with the wolf, may be realized.

However, the hopes for lasting peace in the world remained a dream and were never realized. Soon the people started building the Tower of Babel, with the intention of reaching heaven. The reason for undertaking such a stupendous construction as this is explained by the Sipurnu. They planned to crown a king in that city who would have supreme power to dictate and rule all the world. Although they had conceived an impossible scheme, the Lord had to intervene and scatter them. Even had they continued their work for an unlimited time, they would never have attained their goal. The answer is given from which we can learn the strength of unity. Unity possesses a great force that even an Utopia, if united may achieve something, will eventually cause harm beyond repair.

Therefore, the intervention was necessary. There is a moral in that story from which we can see and learn how powerful and effective unity can be when effected for real and true purpose. But unfortunately, falsehood and treachery are solidly united, whereas those who are fighting for truth are dispersed and divided.

Around the Tents of Torah

LECH LECHA

"Get thee out of thy country – to the land which I will show thee." The commentators have already remarked that the expression "Lecha" (literally "to thee") seems to be on the surface of it unnecessary. The following explanation may, however, be advanced. The departure of Abraham from his birthplace to a destination which the Lord will show him, was one of the tests by which the Lord tested him. It was done with the intention of strengthening the faith of Abraham in the Lord. When a Jew seeks to deepen and to strengthen his faith, this is termed "goer". He progresses and advances in his faith and conviction in the Almighty. He elevates himself from a lower degree in belief to a higher and loftier standard in faith. Moreover, he goes, as it were, to himself, to his holy source and spiritual origin.

According to the Rabbis, every Jew is by nature a believer. They have told us that even a sinner is full of mitzvot even as a pomegranate is full of seeds which are embedded deeply in the fruit. Similarly, faith is embedded deeply in the heart of every Jew. Similarly, a Chassidic Rabbi has said that in every Jewish heart is engraved the Ten Commandments, but the dust of life sometimes covers up the letters and makes them invisible. Occasionally, however, when a holy wind blows the holy writings are revealed again in their full glory.

Thus the transgressor is considered as one who would run away from himself. From the image of the Lord, in which he was created while believing in the Lord he goes to himself. That is why the Lord told Abraham "lech lecha", "go to you", to the origin of holiness.

The Yalkut comments, said Rabbi Brachiah, "Our father Abraham was compared to a bottle of perfume which was hermetically sealed and left lying in a corner; smell remained inside the bottle. But as soon as it was opened, the pleasant smell came out. So the Lord said to Abraham: 'Move yourself from place to place and your name will become famous'." This interpretation contains an important thought.

It is an historical fact that when our people are living in peace and tranquillity in an affluent society, they indulge in the pleasures of life, with all its banalities. It is then that the perfume of our Torah is left lying in an obscure corner, unattended and neglected. We are not seeking ways and means to increase and further the influence of our Torah upon the youth. We are sitting with folded arms forgetting our duties towards Judaism. However, as soon as we are forced to be on the move, because of internal or external pressures, then our greatness reveals itself. We are prepared to bring sacrifices for our faith. That was exactly the duty of Abraham, to educate humanity during his wanderings and travels.

"I will make your name great." The Yalkut narrates that Abraham had issued coins, on one side of which was engraved an old man and an old woman, and on the reverse side, a boy and a girl. This was intended to emphasize an important truth – that old people have to be respected and honoured. The young person of today is the old man of tomorrow. At that time brute force was respected. They did not believe in the existence of a soul and in morality. Their custom was to push the old and disabled down from a high mountain in order to be rid of them. Therefore, Abraham depicted old people and young on the same coin, to teach his generation the mitzva of honouring the old.

In our daily prayers we mention the "shield of Abraham". Abraham was given such a prominent place in our prayers because he was prepared to sacrifice his life for his faith. Therefore, the signal honour was given to him.

We also call our Torah the "Torah of Moses", because he also sacrificed his life for our Torah. Many a time he was insulted and abused and yet he never lost his faith.

(Verse 8) "Beth-El to the west and Ai to the east. And he built there (Abraham), an altar to the Lord and he called in the name of the Lord." The duty of a Jew is to proclaim the name of the Lord at all times, in the morning and evening, namely, in youth and in old age. Evening is the evening of life. "Our help and salvation will come from the Lord," as King David has said, "and our belief in the nights", which refers to old age. In the same way the morning – the last – is symbolical. This is when we are prosperous and young, our personal sun is rising as it were. Then too we have to believe and pray to the Lord. Abraham had fulfilled this during his lifetime at all times, in his youth and old age. Moreover, he had also tried to spread his beliefs to other people.

Nevertheless, his nephew Lot revolted against Abraham. He desired to live a free life, without any duties and obligations, as it is written: "And he raised his eyes and saw that the land of Sdom is full of waters." "Waters" implies wealth and luxury.

He subsequently started an argument, but Abraham warned him, "let there not be any arguments between us, as the Prizi is dwelling in the land." Abraham admonished Lot, saying "why should we argue? Do not you see the Prizi? He is our common enemy who wants to destroy us. Therefore, we have to live in unity, to meet the common danger, or our power of resistance will be diminished."

However, Lot remained adamant and went to stay in Sdom.

During the war between the kings, Lot was captured, and he then turned to Abraham for help. Abraham the Ivri was told about Lot's predicament. The reason why Abraham was called "the Ivri" is explained by Rabbi Yehuda as follows: Ever, in Hebrew, means "a side", implying that the whole world is on one side, and we are on the other side. We have our own system of religious life and observe the commandments and laws of our Torah, while the rest of the world have their specific religion. We do not interfere with them, but some of them disturbed and persecuted us. They did not want to understand and recognise our way of life and our historical aspirations to dwell in peace and tranquillity in our land.

Abraham was told that his brother, Lot, had been captured. The Yalkut remarks that actually he was not Abraham's brother, but because they had the same appearance they were called brothers.

The following story appears in the same source. After Lot had been captured by the Kings, they led him around in order to deceive and mislead the people. Due to the fact that they looked alike, many thought that he was Abraham, and flocked to listen to him and were surprised to hear him urging them to worship idols. They thought therefore that Abraham had denounced his belief in the Lord. Abraham realised the grave danger to his belief and therefore hurried to save Lot, which was a matter of extreme urgency. The Lord helped him and he succeeded in saving his nephew.

The King of Sdom suggested to Abraham that he give him the persons and take the goods for himself. But Abraham refused and replied: "I will not take from a thread even to a shoelace." Rava remarked that because Abraham refused to take anything from the King of Sdom, his children were rewarded with two mitzvot, the blue thread in the Tzitzit and the strap of the Tephillin.

What is the connection between them? It may be explained that the King of Sdom offered to Abraham to take the wealth and the people he would take. To that offer Abraham refused and suggested otherwise, that he give Abraham the souls and the wealth would go to the King. "Look," he said to the King of Sdom, "I conquered the Kings with a small army. I believed in the Lord, and was not afraid to engage them in battle. In the meantime what has happened to the wealth of Lot? He became poor overnight, as he had lost everything. The soul cannot be conquered, as the spirit lives on forever. However, it needs continual strengthening which is accomplished by the fulfilment of the mitzvot. The putting on of

Tephillin cements our faith. We offer all our faculties to the service of the Lord. All our deeds and thoughts are directed towards the Almighty. Similarly the mitzvah of Tzitzit, indicated to that effect, as it says: "And you will remember the mitzvot of the Lord." We have to serve the Lord with self-sacrifice. That was Abraham's reply, that he never wanted any material possessions, and that he preferred spiritual attainments, which are the Tephillin and the Tzitzit.

VAYERA

(18-1) "And the Lord appeared to him as he sat at the tent door in the heat of the day." The name of Abraham is not mentioned; the text merely states "appeared unto him".

The reason may be as follows: Our Rabbis have learned from here the importance of visiting the sick. The Lord has set an example to future generations to visit the sick. Thus if the text would have stated "to Abraham" some would have inferred from it that here was an exceptional instance. Abraham was a very important, holy and exceptional personality; he has to be visited. However, when the sufferer is not so important, then the mitzvah may be overlooked. The text, therefore, merely states "appeared to him", to emphasize an important point, that the mitzvah is not confined to any particular, special person. It has to be fulfilled to anybody, regardless of status or importance.

The Talmud states that by visiting the sufferer, the sickness diminishes by a sixtieth. The reason for this may be logically explained in the light of the advice given by our sages on how to render the visit most effective and beneficial to the ailing person. We are to cheer him up by pleasant conversation, to assist him by good advice and render him any service that is wanted to inspire him with hope and fighting spirit. The sufferer will then feel uplifted and, above all, wanted and encouraged.

When Jacob became ill, his son Joseph hurried from his palace to be near his father, with immediate and positive results (Gen. 18-2).

Rav Bima says that "he who visits the sick is greatly rewarded". The fruit he enjoys in this world while the stock remains for him for the world to come.

Visiting the sick may truly be considered as a humanitarian and unselfish gesture. It brings people nearer to one another, and contributes towards a strong and everlasting friendship. Its immeasurable value will remain imprinted forever upon the mind of the sufferer. While the Lord was visiting him, Abraham lifted his eyes and saw three men. He ran from the tent door to meet them and left the Lord. From that biblical fact our Rabbis have come to a very fundamental conclusion (Shabat 127).

The receiving of visitors stands higher than the receiving of the Lord. Superficially this is difficult to understand, but the statement really contains a deeper meaning. Normally people pray and respect the Lord because we expect rewards of longevity, riches and happiness. But when we invite a guest, a stranger who is a pauper, we have to do it for no ulterior motives or reason. It has to be executed and carried out for the sake of love, of humanity.

Abraham perceived the three men who appeared like simple rustics; yet he ran towards them with great enthusiasm and warmth to invite them to his home. So that is the deeper meaning of the statement, we have to receive guests with kindness, without any expectation of reward. The Lord rewards those who show love and mercy to the poor and strangers.

The Midrash states: The Lord provided the people of Israel with water and bread in the desert as a reward for the water and bread which Abraham gave to the angels.

Around the Tents of Torah

The Talmud makes an amazing remark (Bava Metzia 86) that women are not so keen to receive guests! When Abraham told Sarah to prepare ordinary flour for her guests she gave fine flour. How can this example be quoted: in fact it proves the reverse. She actually provided better food than she was asked to by her husband.

The answer is as follows: actually women are kind and good hearted and as keen to receive guests as are men. Yet there is one basic difference – women are house proud – they are trying to keep their reputation as good home-makers, and are afraid that an over-critical visitor may cause their reputations to suffer. She exerts herself to make everything perfect as far as all arrangements are concerned. From her over-anxiety she becomes nervous and eventually reluctant to receive guests. Sarah affords an example of this. Abraham ordered ordinary flour but she had to prepare the best. This over-anxiety accounts for not being so keen to invite guests. There is an additional explanation of the statement by our sages to the effect that it is greater to receive guests than to receive the Lord.

Our Rabbis have told us that whenever there is peace in the house there also rests the presence of the divine so a person may reason it is better not to invite guests in order to avoid arguments with his wife, so the presence of the Lord will remain in the house. Thus the Rabbis have commanded us in spite of everything, invite guests and do not worry in that event about the presence of the Lord.

The angels came to announce to Abraham the destruction of Sdom. On hearing of the impending destruction of Sdom Abraham started to intercede on their behalf by pleading for mercy. He humbled himself before the Lord by saying: "I am dust and ash!" These two terms contain two aspects of humbleness. Dust has no past but it possesses the ingredients of a future; it may be used in buildings and in construction. Ash on the other hand, has a past. When a building is consumed the ashes remain but it has no future, very little can be done with ash. Abraham humbles himself and says CT am worthless in the presence of the Lord, I have neither past nor future", said Rava (Sota 17).

As a reward to Abraham who has humbled himself before the Lord by saying "I am dust and ash", his children were rewarded with two mitzvot, the dust of the sota and the ash of the Red Heifer – Para Aduma.

Many commentators have been puzzled by the association. What is a "Sota"? When a married woman was suspected by her husband of committing adultery she was named "sota", meaning either foolishness or turning away from the correct path of purity. Even when her innocence was proved, if her behaviour was still of a foolish nature and manner, which warranted gossip about her, her husband was moved to stern action against her. The Talmud states that when a person is tempted to commit a sin, he has to remind himself that he came from dust and will return to dust – that thought will eventually sober him up, it will serve as an anchor upon his sinful thoughts. Had the woman who acted in an immodest manner, which does not befit a Jewess, thought soberly and asked herself the vital question "where am I coming from, and where am I going?" she would certainly have been humbled. Therefore in her meal offering, dust had to be added in order to remind her not to act foolishly again.

When a person comes into contact with a human corpse he becomes unclean for seven days. On the third and seventh day the water mixed with the ash of the red heifer which was slaughtered and burned, was sprinkled in order to cleanse him.

When he is alive it is natural for man to boast and act egotistically and claim that he is the supreme act of creation. However, when he is dead he contaminates and spreads diseases more than an animal does. The reason is simple: the greatness and importance of a person lies in his soul; physically, animals are mightier than men.

The prophet Jeremiah (9-22) has already emphasised "Neither let the mighty man glory in his might". A person has to be humble and meek. The ash which was used for cleansing the person has reminded him of his unimportance and insignificance. Ash has no future so your exaggerated pride and egotism has no future.

(19-27) "And Abraham got up early in the morning."

In Brachot 19 our Rabbis state that our prayers were established by our Patriarchs. Abraham established the morning prayer, Isaac the afternoon prayer and Jacob the evening prayer. These prayers correspond to the periods in which our Patriarchs lived and exerted their influence and authority.

The period in which Abraham lived was the beginning, the sunrise of our faith and history. He had to struggle and fight hard in order to spread and propagate his religious ideas. The expression in the Bible "And Abraham rose in the morning" describes correctly the mood of the time, he could not afford to tarry or to waver as it might be too late. Thus he had to be early, the prayer of Shacharit, morning prayer, is attributed to him. Isaac's life was stable and tranquil. He represented the afternoon. The sun is shining, nature is smiling, everything seems contented and happy.

His way of prayer is described in the Bible – "and Isaac went out to meditate in the field among the flowering and green meadows, there he found the nearness to the Lord". He was at peace with himself and with the world. It is the prayer of joy. The prophet Eli was answered through the prayer of Mincha which is the prayer of joy. Jacob, who had the most depressing and difficult life, established the evening prayer – Maariv. From his early youth until his old age his years were filled with tragedies and strife. Unlike the others he died in a strange land, in Egypt. (22-11) "And he lighted upon a place and tarried there all night." It was the sunset – clouds of darkness had descended upon him. However, even at the desperate period of his life he never gave up hope, he prayed and was saved.

(202-12) And the Lord remembered Sara as he had said and the Lord did unto Sarah as he had spoken. And Sarah conceived and bore Abraham a son. The Talmud in Rosh Hashana 11 states that Sarah, Rachel and Chana have conceived on Rosh Hashana. Rabbi Eliezer proves it from various Biblical sources. It may be well explained allegorically. We say in our prayers on Rosh Hashana that the world was created on that day, that was the physical beginning. Rabbi Eliezer adds that it was also the spiritual beginning, namely the three pillars of our faith were conceived on that day – Isaac, Joseph and Samuel.

Isaac was the pillar of prayer, it was his blessing which he bestowed upon Jacob that had the desired effect. We have survived all those tribulations and returned to Israel.

Joseph, in spite of the cruel deed perpetrated by his brothers against him by selling him for a slave, did not remain bitter for long. It did not influence his faith. He constantly proclaimed his faith, consequently he saved his family from famine. Finally he was instrumental in the survival of our people.

By anointing David at the risk of his life, Samuel assured the continuity of Israel. It is our basic belief that Messiah will be a descendant of King David. Moreover it was those mothers who were responsible for the greatness and achievements of their children. The effectiveness of Sarah as an educator and guide to her son was corroborated by the Lord. "Everything that Sarah will say you will have to listen to her". Similarly Rachel took away the idol from her father Laban as she was afraid that it might influence her children. The prophet Jeremiah emphasised and underlined that thought in the most eloquent expression: "Rachel is crying over her children". Even from her grave she worries and laments over the fate of her children. She feels responsible for them and for their future.

Likewise Chana watched, cared and sacrificed her life for her son Shmuel to bring him up in the most holy and righteous manner. She left him in the holy Temple to imbibe the sanctity of the surroundings. On her part it constituted a great personal sacrifice as she would have liked to have him near her to embrace and to love him. Moreover she thought more of his future which is the ideal way of bringing up children.

CHAYEI-SARA

The sidra of Chayei-Sara is based on the theme of youth education.

The Yalkut relates this story about Rabbi Akiva. While he was lecturing to his disciples he noticed to his disappointment that some of his audience were nodding and falling asleep. In order to awaken them, he exclaimed: "Do you know the reason why Esther ruled over 127 countries? Because Sarah lived 127 years!" The question is obvious, indeed the facts are true but what is the association between these two numbers?

The story may be explained allegorically. Rabbi Akiva, who lived during the time of the Roman occupation, observed with horror and grief the spiritual apathy and lethargy which prevailed among the people of Israel. So he reminded them of our glorious past and referred particularly to Esther, who had endangered her life in order to save her people. She knew exactly the hazards she would have to face, and related them to Mordechai. She had not been invited by the king, and if she would enter the palace uninvited, she might be sentenced to death. Nonetheless, she went and succeeded.

However, whence did she draw that spiritual courage and strength to take this course of action which endangered her life? Rabbi Akiva gave the answer. It was her proper religious upbringing in school and above all her home background, as is written in Esther (chapt. 2-1): "And he brought up Hadassa

(Esther)". The text uses here the expression "omen", which also means to be an expert, implying that the upbringing of a child requires the services of a highly specialised and competent person.

With reference to Sarah, the text says she lived a hundred years, twenty years and seven years. Rashi remarks "Why the repetition of the word years?" Rashi renders the following answer. She was pure and honest at the age of a hundred as she was at the age of twenty. She constantly maintained and upheld a high standard of honesty and purity. Sara had indeed a hard and exacting life. She partnered her husband in all his tribulations and vicissitudes which were plenty. She educated and guided her son and watched over him jealously. For that she attained the highest praise from the L-rd. The L-rd told Abraham: "Everything that Sarah tells you, you have to listen to her." Rashi comments that she possessed the divine spirit. Esther tried to emulate the life of Sarah. She looked up to her as her spiritual guide and mentor. Sarah it is to be remembered, she also endangered her life when she went down to Egypt.

After Sarah's death Abraham tried to find a wife for his son Isaac. He entrusted his manager, Eliezer, with that mission. He instructed him to go to Aram-Naharaim to look for a wife for his son, but made it clear to him, "my son will not settle there. He must stay in the land of Canaan". Following up the teaching of Sarah, he remembered her words that even a grown up child must be looked after. Thus he was afraid to let him stay in Aram in case he might be influenced by the evil environment.

He must stay in Canaan under his constant vigilance. Eliezer came to Aram. He stopped at a well of water where he made a sign – "And let it come to pass that the damsel to whom I shall say, Let down thy pitcher, I pray thee, that I may drink and she will say drink and I will give thy camels to drink also. Let the same be that Thou hast appointed for thy servant, Isaac, as a wife and thereby shall I know that Thou hast shown kindness unto my master."

Actually we, the people of Israel, are not allowed signs. What he really made was a test of character, which actually counts in the success of married life. He wanted to ascertain whether she was kind-hearted and good-natured. Rivka could have said after all: "I am a lady and you cannot expect me to provide water for you and especially as you are older". However, Rivka helped him and his camels with water. Rivka proved to be the ideal partner to Isaac. Later on she continued the teaching of Sara and Abraham and she imbued her children with love for our religion. She also emphasised the important principle: "Bring up your child! Do not rely upon others to do it for you!"

TOLDOT

"And these are the generations of Isaac, Abraham's son. Abraham begot Isaac." The Targum – Yerushalmi, adds: "And this is the pedigree of his birth", implying that Isaac felt it as a privilege, and proclaimed it humbly, that he was the son of Abraham who was the first to recognise the existence of the Lord. In doing so, Isaac fulfilled the commandment, "Honour your father", as he showed his pride in the greatness and holiness of his famous father.

However, it is implicit that the son had to continue in the ways of his father, so that the latter should also be satisfied with the son. The children have to be "a crown to their parents" (Prov. 17), so it is also stated that "Abraham begot Isaac", showing that he also was pleased with the worthiness of his son.

"And Isaac was forty years old when he took Rebecca" (Verse 20). Our Rabbis in Megilla (10) have already stated that wherever it uses the expression in the Bible "And it was", it implies "grief". Isaac also was grieved because he could not find a suitable and respectable wife in his birthplace Canaan. He was forced to seek a life-companion in a far-away place, as in Canaan the people were idol worshippers.

"And the children struggled within her" (22). Rashi comments that when Rivka, who was pregnant, passed a place of Torah learning, Jacob wanted to go out, whereas when she passed a place of idol worship, Esau desired to do so.

Actually what did compel our Rabbis to explain the verse in that manner? It was already stated by the "Mesech Chochma" that a boy at his birth is called in Hebrew "Zachar" and not "Ben". "Ben" denotes one who is already a mature person. Here the verse states "Habanim" (the sons). Therefore, Rashi came to the conclusion that it does not refer to the present, but to the future when they will grow up an uncompromising religious disagreement will prevail between them. The animosity will be so great and unbridgeable, that even if Jacob were to assimilate he would not be accepted as the religious hatred stems and originates as it were from birth.

This contradicts the false theory of assimilation, that if we shall deny our origin, we shall be accepted with open arms by Esau. History has proved otherwise. Even to his own brother from birth, Esau will not change his attitude and relationship towards Jacob. It is an eternal struggle until the coming of messiah. Naturally, there are also exceptions. The Yalkut mentions that Rabbi Yehuda the Prince and a Roman, Antoninus, ate at the same table.

Rivka was very grieved about the continuous strife between the two brothers. The Rabbis Shem and Ever, explained to her that it is the eternal battle between the good and evil. It is the division between the snake which causes death to humanity and the tree of life, which brings happiness and contentment to people. It is the struggle between the lion and the lamb. It will be Elijah who will announce the eternal peace to humanity.

Esau is ruddy as a premonition of his love for hunting, the shedding of blood and murder. He is covered with hair, implying that his intentions and thoughts are covered with a layer of lies and hypocrisy. Jacob was a quiet man, dwelling in tents. Tents, in the plural is explained by Sipurnu thus: one tent he used for his shepherd's needs and the other was used for a place of worship, when he prayed to the Lord. For Jacob, spiritual needs and requirements were as necessary as material and physical values.

Esau was a hunter. He possessed the capability to hunt and to deceive and indeed he succeeded in misleading his father, who believed that Esau was a righteous person. However, he failed to do so with his mother, Rivka. She recognised his nature and evil intentions. The reason is simple. Isaac was by nature a saint, a holy person, who knew nothing of the falsehood and degradations of humanity. He believed everyone. It had never entered his mind that people will tell lies and certainly his son will not deceive him. Therefore, he was proud of Esau and of all the various questions which he asked him about religion. He accepted them at their face value, without any criticism or doubt.

Rivka, on the other hand, had a brother Lavan, who was a compulsive liar, who always evaded the truth. So because of her upbringing in an untruthful environment, she started to observe more closely and to scrutinize the actions and deeds of her son, Esau. She came to a very sad conclusion, namely that her own son is a liar.

Furthermore, our Rabbis (Yalkut 28) have stated that women are more observant about the character of people than men. Therefore, she loved and appreciated Jacob, who was indeed a kind and sincere person. Esau was the first born and in those days the first born was supposed to be a holy person. Jacob noticed that Esau's unethical behaviour did not warrant his occupying such an important position as this. His expression was the words of a glutton, when he said to Jacob "Feed me!" The Talmud tells in Psochim (30) (in Eiruvin

65) that the manner of speaking of a person reveals his character. Therefore, Jacob decided to buy the first-born rights from Esau. (31) "And said Jacob, sell me as today your birthright."

Jacob was afraid that at a later date, he may possibly change his mind. He therefore emphasised that one should always remember one's state of mind and one's promises of today. Jacob, however, was certain that Esau would remain constantly at the same low spiritual level. Esau agreed to the proposal.

(32) "And Esau said: 'Behold I am at the point to die and what profit shall this birthright do to me?'" Here we see the fundamental difference between Esau and Jacob. To Jacob death reminds him of penitence and expressions of regret, as our Rabbis have said: "Return one day before your death." Esau did not believe in a coming world. He was concerned mainly with this world, so he wanted to get rid of his birthright, which promised rewards in which he did not believe. So Esau despised his birthright. According to our law in Deuteronomy (21-17), a first-born son gets a double portion in the inheritance. However, the Ibn-Ezra stated that Isaac was a poor person, thus Esau could not profit by his privileges as a first born, therefore he despised everything.

Owing to the hunger which prevailed in the land of Israel he went to Philistia, but the Lord told him to remain in the land as its rightful owner. Then the Lord told him to stay in the land as a stranger (3-26), which, on the face of it, is a contradiction.

This may be explained as follows: the Lord advised him how he should conduct himself at the moment in the land. Although the land did not belong to him, and he was a stranger, he should act like the owner, build the country as, eventually, he would be the owner of the land. The farmer who tills the fields is the master of the land.

Unfortunately, Isaac lingers on. He does not return immediately to the land. So the Lord gives him a bitter taste of what it means to be a stranger in a strange land.

Isaac works diligently, he reopens the wells of water which belonged to his father Abraham, and though officially he is a citizen of the land, the Philistines filled them up. Isaac gives three names to the wells:

(1) Esek – Contention
(2) Sitna – enmity
(3) Rehoboth – There is room.

The expression Esek refers to financial matters (Levi 19).

Some maintain that the source and cause of hatred of the Jew in the diaspora is the belief of our enemies that we dominate the business sphere and lead the capitalistic system. This is untrue. Their hatred is blind, without any reason and foundation. In our times six million of our brethren were massacred in cold blood. It is crude, wild hatred.

But when he came to Israel, there was room for him; he recognised the importance of having a land where he is the master of his destiny. For that he thanked the Lord.

From the beginning of the Creation of the world, a feud was started between brothers (Yalkut Gen. 38) Cain and Abel. "The one said the holy Temple must be built in my place", whilst the other opposed him and claimed that "in my boundary it should be erected". Each one proclaimed that his belief was the correct one, which resulted in bloodshed. Esau wanted to kill his brother, but Rivka's wisdom and advice saved him. She had managed to confound and mislead Esau who geared himself and strove to acquire the blessing of his father, not because he believed in it, but by this means he would be able to deceive and mislead people in believing him to be a righteous and honest person. The proof would be "Look, my father, who is a saint, honours and singles me out as his darling son!"

Rivka exactly knew his evil intentions, his hidden and hypocritical ulterior motives, and therefore advised Jacob how to obtain the blessings. Isaac blessed Jacob: "Therefore the Lord give thee of the dew of the heaven and the fatness of the earth." (27-28) Firstly he mentions heaven, which refers to holiness and spirituality, which descend from above, and then automatically one will acquire the "fatness of the earth", the material assets which will enable him to support the poor and the needy.

Esau came in after Jacob left and announced: "I am your firstborn son, Esau." Isaac trembled exceedingly. He now began to realise what vicious hatred prevailed between his two sons. He was very much afraid for the future as animosity between the brothers was more dangerous and tragic than hatred between strangers. The results could be fatal, and Isaac said: "Your brother came with subtlety." The Targum translates "with wisdom". The text says "mirma", which actually means "falsehood and slyness". Why is it then that the Targum translated it "with wisdom"?

The answer is that perhaps Isaac's reply has a double meaning. He says to Esau: "My dear son, according to your moral standards, a person who can deceive and bluff, is a clever person, then naturally, Jacob is a clever man, but according to my conception, Jacob came with subtlety."

At the end Isaac blessed Esau, but the hatred became stronger and deeper. It had become a great flame and very dangerous. Indeed, Esau loved and honoured his father, therefore he waited for the death of his father, when he would be able to carry out his brutal schemes so Rivka advised Jacob to escape. Before his departure, the latter wanted a special blessing which would be directed to him only. Isaac understood now the real position and blessed him with the blessing of Abraham, who had likewise given the blessing to Isaac only, and had excluded Ishmael who grew up to be a wild man who did not appreciate blessings.

VA'ETZEH

(28-10) "And Jacob went out from Beersheba". The Yalkut asks a very good question: Jacob was at this time in Hebron, so why does the text mention Beersheba?

The answer is given as follows: "Sheva" in Hebrew is an oath, so the meaning would be that he left the place where many oaths were given. Avimelech gave an oath to Abraham that he would remain truthful to him. Esau also gave an oath to Jacob that he would remain satisfied with the selling of the first-born rights.

There is a deep thought in this interpretation. Jacob realised the fallacy of believing in promises, declarations and even oaths of strangers. Avimelech made a promise to Abraham that he would help and support him, and then made a reversal and became an enemy. Esau promised and gave an oath that the first-born right meant nothing to him and later wanted to kill his brother. So Jacob decided not to trust any longer the mere lip service of strangers, who are like broken reeds, but to rely on the Lord only!

At this time he established the "Maariv", the evening prayer. (11) "And he lighted upon a certain place and tarried there all night, because the sun was set." His spiritual position was in a state of sunset. He fled from Esau to the unknown of Lavan, about whom he had already heard not very encouraging reports.

Nevertheless, he has trust in his prayer, which will help him in his predicament, and will extricate him from darkness to light. The Lord will save him from evil and misery. The soil of the land of Israel is very dear to him; he does not expect or desire riches or luxuries. He is satisfied with stones for pillows, falls asleep with pleasant and sweet dreams.

(12) "And he dreamed, and behold, a ladder set up on the earth, and the top of it reached to heaven, and behold the angels of the Lord ascending and descending on it." Actually, why is a ladder necessary

for angels? They are able to fly with their wings as the prophet Yehezkel has seen them in his vision (chap. 1). The implication is that a person cannot attain, in one leap, to a very high spiritual level. There is, rather, a gradual process of very hard and strenuous effort and concentration, until one may eventually reach it – "its top reached to heaven".

We are standing on the earth, but we have to strive to greater spiritual heights, to holiness and to perfection. For that, we have to take an example from the ladder. The ladder could not stand firmly on the ground unless it was supported by the heavens. Similarly, a person cannot remain strongly implanted in his own strength and might, unless he is helped and supported by the Lord. Indeed, in his dream, Jacob sees wonderful visions. The Lord promises him (15) "And behold I am with thee and will keep thee whithersoever thou goest."

(16) "And Jacob awaked out of his sleep and he said: 'Surely the Lord is in this place: and I knew it not?'" The question may be asked: how did Jacob come to the conclusion that the place was holy?

The answer may perhaps be given as follows: In the Talmud (Brachot 56) Rav Shmuel, the son of Nachmoni, said, in the name of Rav Yehonatan. A person dreams in the night whatever he thinks during the day. On that day several frightening events had occurred to Jacob. He had fled from Esau, then according to our Rabbis, his nephew, Elifaz, the son of Esau, pursued, caught him and wanted to kill him, so Jacob gave him all his money to placate him. His intention was to go to Lavan. He has already heard about the trickery of Lavan, his greediness and lust for money. Now he will have to face him as a pauper standing with his head down and begging eyes. He may chase him away. These sad thoughts were certainly fleeting through the mind of Jacob while he was walking and meditating about his uncertain future.

Therefore, his dreams should have been about murder, attacks and poverty. However, he dreams about other things – a ladder and angels; about which he had not thought the whole day. He, therefore, came to the conclusion that the ground was holy. In similar vein we may interpret a verse in Kohelet (5-11) "Sweet is the sleep of a labouring man, whether he eat little or much, but the satiety of the rich will not suffer him to sleep." The poor labourer works hard the whole day. Various thoughts pass through his mind; if only a miracle would happen and he would become rich. Then he would be able to live comfortably in luxury and style in a spacious house, to give to his children the correct education, to clothe them properly and so on. So when he falls asleep he dreams about riches, his family is happy and contented. He has a luxurious home, beautiful, modern clothes for everyone, thus he sleeps in sweetness and happiness.

About the rich our Rabbis have said, "the more possessions, the more worry". All day he worries that robbers may attack him, the creditors won't pay him, his fortunes may be diminished. Therefore, when he falls asleep, he dreams he is attacked, robbed, the creditors bankrupt. Therefore, he cannot sleep owing to worry, aggravation and disappointment which fill his dreams. In the same context may also be understood the text in Brachot (56) "If one dreams that he is riding on an ox that augurs well for him, but if one dreams that the ox is riding on him, it is a bad sign."

Every human being consists of two parts, namely the spiritual and physical, the soul and the body. The physical part is the animal portion which entices him to attack, damage and to do evil like the wild ox, whereas the spiritual guides him to be good, to have mercy, be kind-hearted and understanding. Thus if he dreams that he is riding on the ox, that is a proof that while he was awake he thought about good deeds, to be charitable, helpful and friendly. That is a good sign as he has chosen the right path in life. But if he dreams that the ox is riding on him, that corroborates the fact that during the day he thought of being wicked, of harming others. He has chosen the wrong way in life.

It also states in Brachot (56) "Said Rav Hanan: These are the objects which one sees in dreams that symbolise peace – a river, a bird and a pot." Water is the essence of unity. When millions of drops of water gather in one place, they become a force, whereas individually they remain ineffective and impotent. Similarly, birds which are migrating from the cold countries to a warmer climate are flying in the company of thousands and more; individually they would not have had the energy and strength to reach their distant destination. It is the unity which gives them the extra ability to overcome all the difficulties which are inherent in the elements of nature. The pot unites water with fire. If one dreams about them it is a sign that during the day he had entertained thoughts about unity and love for people. So that is the reason why Jacob exclaimed: "This is the house of the Lord".

That dream encouraged Jacob and gave him extra belief that he would succeed in his hard road which lay ahead of him. And Jacob made a promise saying, "If the Lord will be with me and I will return in peace to the house of my father … of all thou shall give me I will give a tenth to you". In this verse the expression "B'Shalom" is difficult to understand. The Yalkut (149) states that "B'Shalom" is said to dead persons, whereas to living persons we say "L'Shalom" and here Jacob said "B'Shalom".

There is a reason for this distinction. The letter Lamed in "L'Shalom" emphasises progress and achievements. While a person is alive, he has the capability to advance and acquire spiritual values through the study of the Torah and the fulfilment of the Commandments. But a dead person is absolved from mitzvot. He gets rewarded for the mitzvot which he has carried out in this world. Following up on that explanation, we may now understand why Jacob used the expression "B'Shalom". Jacob knew exactly the nature of Lavan and the place which was a town of idol-worshippers. In a hostile environment like that it is difficult to advance in belief and knowledge. Therefore, he did not ask the maximum from the Lord. He was satisfied to remain static, not to descend from his present spiritual position, at least not to forget what he had learned from his father and teachers. So he prayed that the Lord should help him to remain with his present wisdom and faith in the Almighty. This is what is meant by the expression "B'Shalom", to maintain in the future his religious beliefs.

The end of the verse is also difficult to understand. It sounds that he makes a condition and business transaction with the Lord. He says if the Lord will be with him and make him rich, then he will be willing to give a tenth of his riches to the Lord. So it follows that if the Lord will not enrich him then he will give nothing, which, naturally, is not the case with Jacob.

The answer is as follows: Jacob prayed that his faith in the Lord should be so strong and convincing that even when he would be wealthy he would not say, "My strength and my might has gone and achieved all that". As Moses has warned (Deut. 15-32): "But Jeshurem waxed fat and wicked thou art waxed fat." So actually it was not a condition, but a prayer that the Lord should help him in maintaining his faith at all times and he would then certainly give him charity.

VAYISHLACH

Jacob returned home to Israel. He knew that he would have to meet Esau, his brother who wanted to kill him. In his heart he hoped that after the lapse of so many years Esau's anger might have disappeared and his brother might have become more friendly disposed towards him.

Esau had now become a wealthy, respected person and advanced in years, so his wrath might conceivably have disappeared.

He sends messengers to Esau and instructs them to say: "So you will say to my master Esau ... " Whenever the Bible uses this phrase, it implies that no additions or subtractions are to be made to the statements. This was also the opening sentence by the prophets. Jacob was afraid that the messengers might not carry out their mission exactly by subtracting or adding words. They knew the character of Jacob as being undaunted and fearless and suddenly he subdues and humbles himself by saying "So said your slave Jacob". They might therefore omit that sentence.

Jacob, however, wanted to live in peace and harmony with his brother, so he humbled himself. He continues with Lavan: "I dwelt there, I was a stranger and a shepherd, I led a hard and poor life, longing all the time to return home."

But Lavan prevented it by delegating to him strenuous and difficult tasks. Rashi adds that he had also said to Esau: "I dwelt with Lavan and observed the 613 commandments".

Why was it necessary for him to know whether he observed the commandments? The reason is that Esau suspected that Jacob was not sincere in his beliefs. He accused him of being a cunning hypocrite who hid himself under the camouflage of religion. Thus he let him know that even at the place of Lavan where most of the people were idol worshippers, and where, consequently, to be an observant Jew was a hardship, he yet observed the commandments.

"And I had an ox and ass". The text is in the singular. By that he wanted to placate Esau, who was envious about the blessing. So he said: "Do not be jealous at all my possessions. These I acquired through exertions and worry which are not commensurate with the wealth which I possess. They are like one ass and ox according to my work."

And Jacob feared very much and was distressed. After the L-rd has promised that everything would be in order, why then was he afraid? The answer is that Jacob prepared himself for three eventualities (Yalkut 131), with presents, prayer and war. But afterwards he doubted whether his decision was the correct one. Perhaps it would have been better to declare war immediately and not go with humility and apologies? Maybe the path of peace was the best way out? At this time, therefore, it was not clear to him which way to choose; it was rather slightly confusing and he could not make up his mind. Therefore he "feared and was distressed".

That explains what he said to his messengers (18) "and you will say, your servant Jacob sends you a present to my master Esau, but he is also behind us". He lets him know that he wants to live in peace, but it is not capitulation, "he is also behind us", prepared and ready to fight and to defend his honour and pride and right.

(24) "And Jacob was left alone and there wrestled a man with him". From this we are given to learn that if Jacob remains alone he will find himself in a difficult position. The implication is that if the younger generation does not continue the Judaism and faith of the older generation and will start to wander and deviate on other roads we will have to battle hard to keep our spiritual position intact. In that context may be explained the saying of Rabbi Isaac (Yalkut 132), that a Talmid Chacman, a learned person, may not go alone in the night, implying that if darkness and clouds are covering our spiritual horizon, then he may not go out alone, he may not remain alone nor sit with folded arms. He has to gird himself with all his powers in order to save the deteriorating position.

"He touched the hollow of his thigh." Comments the Yalkut: "He touched the righteous people who will descend from him", as if to say, "do not despair there is still hope, the younger generation may still change their minds and behaviour". And indeed when he meets the Angel of Esau, the sun rises, implying that the youth will return to the true belief which will eventually lead them to the true path of life.

Esau meets Jacob and he asks him "who are these to you?" Jacob answers: "The children which the L-rd has graciously given your servant". (3-5) He has children who are believers in the L-rd, and for that one has to be thankful. We have to pray and ask mercy from the L-rd as we are continually entangled in the strife of life, the fight for existence.

Esau implored that his children should walk together with Jacob's children. Let them play and study in harmony, by which he hopes that eventually Jacob's children would lose their identity. Jacob understood the evil intentions and refused. He continued on his road to Israel. There he wanted to establish himself and build his permanent home. Jacob returned, unaffected by his sojourn in Lavan's environment. He did not forget his Torah nor his faith.

Joseph, however, forgot his home and Torah, remarks the Yalkut, as he says that the L-rd made me forget. There is a fundamental difference between the history of Joseph and Jacob. Jacob fled from his home, but he did not bear any grudges against his family. Even his hatred against Esau he justified secretly in his heart. As Esau had some sort of ground for complaint, therefore he longed for home, hoping everyday to return home. Consequently he continued his studies and tried not to forget them. On the other hand, Joseph was angry with his family for selling him. A salient fact is that even after he became viceroy, he did not communicate with them, which proves the indignation and anger he felt against his family. Anger causes forgetfulness. Also he did not hope to return home, so he did not go over his studies and started to forget.

"And he bought a piece of land." The Yalkut (106) states that there are three places in Israel where we have a legal and historical claim and no other nation can dispute our ownership. The double cave, the grave of Joseph and the Holy Temple, as these places were bought for money. The above three places give us a claim of possession in our land. In the double cave are buried our Patriarchs and Matriarchs who gave us faith, the sense of giving charity and kindness. The Holy Temple is the place where the Divine Presence of the L-rd rested. The grave of Joseph gives us encouragement for our future. In spite of the fact that he was viceroy of Egypt Joseph yet refused to be buried in Egypt. He told his brethren – "the L-rd will remember you and you will carry my bones with you". He had great trust in the future of our people and that trust and confidence he transmitted to us. After he had bought the piece of land, Jacob thought that he would now be able to dwell in peace. Suddenly a great calamity befell him. Schem assaulted his daughter Dina. The brothers immediately retaliated. They avenged the shame of their sister. Jacob became angry with them, saying: "You have troubled me to make me odious unto the inhabitants of the land." To that rebuke the brothers replied: "Should one deal with one's sister as with a harlot?" The discussion and arguments between father and sons contain the two opinions and camps in our nation as regards our attitude towards our oppressors. The one section maintains that despite all the insults and abuses which are thrown at us, we still have to accept them philosophically and make peace with our fate, and remain silent without any resistance. However, the second opinion, mainly that of the younger generation, is that we cannot tolerate and remain silent in face of so many provocations and degradations. They break out in revolution to remedy and revenge the wrongs and cruelty which they have experienced.

VAYESHEV

And Jacob dwelt in the land of his father's sojourning. Our Rabbis have remarked that Jacob wanted to dwell in tranquillity, but he was suddenly beset by the trouble of Joseph.

Jacob had a very strenuous and hard life, so he presumed that at last he could return and live in peace. However, he was rudely awakened by the tragic disappearance of Joseph. Now he started to realise and suspect that somewhere he had failed in his upbringing of his children. This has to be a continuous process from childhood to adolescence with constant vigilance and supervision. Complacency and self-satisfaction were great dangers.

The most harmful and venomous human failing is jealousy which has to be suppressed and eliminated as quickly as possible. Jacob unfortunately was very busy and occupied to manage the interests of Lavan as he says in Gen. 31-38, "the drought consumed me and the frost by night and my sleep fled from mine eyes", so he neglected to penetrate deeply enough into the affairs and relationships of his own children.

It is an effective lesson for posterity and one that parents have to be always on guard against. It repudiates the complacent attitude taken by some parents who exclaim unconcernedly: "I do not interfere in the affairs of my children; they are big enough to look after themselves." Had they taken a more positive approach there would have been less juvenile problems.

Joseph was indeed innocent. He was a victim of circumstances. The jealousy, suspicion and gossip was quoted in the history of their families. Jacob preferred Rachel to Leah, which led the children of Leah to feel unwanted. Then when Jacob met his brother Esau under strained circumstances as Esau threatened to kill him, Rachel and Joseph were placed last out of reach of imminent danger. Other little events have fitted in inadvertently to create a pattern of suspicion. The last straw was the giving of the shirt of many colours to Joseph. There is a common saying that parents love their children like the ten fingers on their hands; but even fingers are not all equal. Jacob loved all his children alike, but Joseph being younger, more delicate and later orphaned, deserved slightly more attention and care, which is an innocent gesture in human behaviour. However, Jacob and Joseph were not aware of the circumstances and the set up of hatred and this resulted in the selling of Joseph.

Joseph is by nature a dreamer, hence he dreams about fields, sheaves, sun, moon and stars. That enrages the brothers even more against him. The first dream did not impress Jacob very much as it was of material concern only. However, the second dream about the heavenly bodies made a deep impression on him. To quote the text "But his father kept the saying in mind". "And Jacob sent him out of the valley of Hebron". Our Rabbis (Sota 11) have remarked that Hebron actually stands on a mountain and not in a valley. The answer may be given as follows: In view of the hatred and animosity which had prevailed among the brothers, spiritually and morally they were in a valley, implying a moral decline and depression of character and ethical behaviour.

They were sinking fast into the valley of tears and grief. Joseph carries out the instructions of his father; he is going to seek his brothers (15). "A certain man found him and behold he was wandering in the field." The word "wandering" aptly describes the state of mind in which Joseph found himself. He was wandering, was at a loss as to what to do, how to act, because he had already noticed how his brothers avoided him, being reluctant even to speak to him. On the other hand, he had to fulfil the instructions of his father. The man asks him what he was seeking? To which Joseph replies briefly in words which are expressive of his character and personality. "I seek my brothers." Indeed it was the theme of Joseph throughout his lifetime. Even after being sold for a share he was neither bitter nor revengeful against his brothers. Had he been so he could have easily punished them for their deeds. But it was against the character of Joseph, who was kind, considerate and forgiving.

After selling him, they slaughtered a he-goat, dipped the coat in blood and sent it to Jacob for recognition. Jacob painfully exclaimed "It is my son's coat, an evil beast has devoured him". Through his prophetical wisdom Jacob has used the right phrase. Men can also be transformed into evil beasts. A brother kills his brother. They tried to comfort him but without success. Jacob the Saint cannot conceive how man who was created in the image of the Lord could desecrate the spark of holiness given to him.

Our sages have said that sin causes sin.

Jehuda who was supposed to be the leader of the brothers made a mistake. He should have resisted and opposed violently the intolerance which prevailed among his brothers.

Had he tried hard, he could perhaps have reconciled them. However, that realisation came too late. Therefore the text says (38-1) "And it came to pass at that time that Juda went down from his brothers", which implies that he "went down" in his wisdom and prestige. Tamar was nearly burnt at the stake because of his haste and wrong attitude adopted by him. An innocent person could have been sentenced to death because of his clumsiness.

Joseph, on the other hand, in spite of being a slave and a stranger, remained calm, sober and faithful to his religion in the face of temptation and enticement. As he says (30-9): "How then can I do this great wickedness and sin against the Lord?" He did not commit the sin, as goodness breeds goodness.

The Midrash narrates the following: Joseph was about to succumb to the temptation of Zlicha and commit the sin but his father's face stopped him from transgression. That may be explained allegorically. Joseph, although being upset with his brothers, loved his father deeply and affectionately. In spite of being young he made up his mind that, prior to all his actions and undertakings, he would ask himself the question: "will my father be pleased with my action or will he be ashamed and repudiate me?" So, when he was under the evil influence of Zlicha, he immediately remembered his promise and asked the vital question: "What will be my father's reaction?" Naturally that stopped him immediately. That proves how much Joseph was devoted to and loved his father. Even being far distant, he did not wish to embarrass him. That may serve as an example to our present generation of how to honour and cherish parents.

CHANUKA

Most of our festivals are associated with lights. We light candles on the eve of Shabbat and Yom Tovim, etc. In Megillat Esther, it is recorded, "to the Hebrews there was light". A logical explanation may be given as follows: our festivals were designed by the Lord to drive away the darkness, despondency and disappointments of life and replace it with rays of hope, joy and happiness. The Midrash provides an interesting reason why women have to light candles. It was Eve, by enticing Adam to eat from the tree of knowledge, who brought death into the world, therefore she has to light candles to make amends for and rectify this historical mistake and short-sightedness by bringing cheerfulness and holiness into the home. The festival of Chanuka is mainly based upon lights and candles – indeed it is known as the festival of lights. It was established in that manner with a special emphasis on enlightenment, decency and human dignity.

A vicious battle was fought between the Hebrews and Greeks. In war the individual human life is not considered. With the help of the Lord we won. However we do not glorify war; we are radically opposed to brutal force.

It has already been said that a battle may be won, but the war can be lost. This the Maccabean wanted to bring forcibly and clearly to the people of Israel: the important message for posterity which was already said by the prophet: "not by might but by the spirit of the Lord". We commemorate the miracle not with military parades but by lighting candles in a demonstrative manner, in front of the window to emphasise our deep belief in spiritual and moral values as were preached by our prophets of old. The candles are lit with a special candle which is called Shamas (Beadle) and has to stand higher than the other candles. We also served humanity throughout many generations as the Shamas brought light and justice to the world. Although we were persecuted, humiliated and oppressed, spiritually we mocked our enemies as we were superior to the oppressor.

MIKETZ

Gen. (41-1): "And it came to pass at the end of full three years that Pharah was dreaming." The commentators have already remarked that the correct expression should have been: "and Pharah dreamt" in the past tense. According to the Midrash (Miketz), Rabbi Yochanan said: "by the wicked people they are standing on their G-d, as it says, and he is standing on the river which was Pharaoh's idol whereas, by the righteous people the Lord stands above them, as it says: 'And the Lord stands on him'" (Gen. 28).

This implies that Pharaoh is a dreamer; he dreams about his ambitions to conquer the world, he has no scruples or mercy or consideration, he kills and destroys everything and everyone who stands in his path. He is warned and asked how he could perpetrate cruelties like these; was he not afraid of the Lord who watches over the deeds of humanity, who would certainly punish him? To that warning he retorts: "There is nothing to be afraid of, I am the Lord and law, no one has the right to interfere in my government and actions."

Rulers like these we encounter also in our present time who have no conscience and feeling of justice and mercy. In every generation we have rulers and dictators who are grabbing and trampling upon the weak and undefended. That is the reason why the text is in the present tense – "And Pharaoh is dreaming" – he is still dreaming. The modern contemporary Pharaoh is still dreaming, scheming and planning how to conquer and subdue the weak and the young. This is not so in the case of the righteous. The Lord stands above him, he subdues his desires and temptations to the will of the Lord who guides his destiny, and whom he has to obey. That is what Joseph said to Pharaoh (41-16): "It is not me; the Lord will give Pharaoh an answer of Peace". Pharaoh dreams how to conquer the world and rule over it with an iron fist through the acquisition of grain, then he will be in a position to op press, to dictate and to suppress other nations and people.

Pharaoh dreams (5): "And behold, seven ears of corn came up upon one stalk rank and good". (6): "And behold seven ears, thin and blasted with the east wind sprang up after them". It is interesting to note that with the good ears the text says "upon one stalk" but not so with the thin ears. There is a thought therein. When there is food in abundance, then love, unity and peace prevails in the land and in the home. The words in "one stalk" describe it clearly. But when the food finishes from the sack then arguments and quarrels begin (Bava Metzia). This idea is also expressed with the dream of the cows: " … and behold there came out of the river seven cows, fat fleshed and well-favoured and they fed in the feed grass". The Targum Onkelos adds, "and they pastured in brotherhood", implying that if there is plenty of food then there is love and brotherhood but God forbid, when there is a famine then revolutions, wars and arguments follow, creating havoc and disaster.

(8) "And Pharaoh awoke; it was a dream. And it came to pass in the morning that his spirit was troubled". While he was asleep his dream troubled and hurt him, but on awaking and realising that everything is but a dream, he felt happy and relaxed. However in the morning when his spirit troubled him, the dream started to oppress him; he was afraid and called for the wise men of Egypt. Joseph interpreted the dream, but Pharaoh did not want to reveal the identity of the interpreter, therefore he changes it to Zophnat-Paneah.

In order to hide the fact that a Hebrew had saved their nation and helped them from the horrors of hunger, and to camouflage his ancestry, Pharaoh gave him Asnat for a wife. Joseph was afraid that he might forget his nation and faith, so he named his first-born son Mnashe for "the Lord made me forget". The Sipurnu adds: "he has forgotten all his tribulations". But Joseph did not want to forget, therefore he called his second son Ephraim. According to the Daat-Zkeinim, he named him after his forefathers Abraham and Isaac, "Eipher", meaning ash, as a reminder of Abraham who had said: "I am dust and ash" and for Isaac who was nearly consumed to ash when he was ready to be brought as a sacrifice.

The brothers came to Egypt to buy food and immediately he jailed Simon. (42-19): "If you are true men one of you will be imprisoned and you will carry corn for the famine of your houses".

Joseph wanted to convince himself whether unity existed among his brothers, if the hatred had disappeared. The imprisonment of one of the brothers would serve as a test and prove whether real love prevailed among them. That could be ascertained through practical deeds but not through empty promises. If one brother would be ready to bring sacrifices for the others, it would be the real and only criterion of unselfish friendship.

About the imprisonment of Simeon the Yalkut (148) narrates an interesting story. All the strong people could not overpower Shimon who was apparently a very strong person, so Joseph sent his son Mnashe to place a chain on his neck and gave him one hard hit. Shiman, being in pain, exclaimed that "the knock comes from my own family". The moral is obvious. An attack which emanates from the family is most painful, menacing and telling, not because of its physical effectiveness, but rather because of its psychological and moral disappointment and grief. Instead of the love and affection that was supposed to prevail there are hatred and animosity. That is the most grievous event which may take place in the life of a person. That was exactly what Joseph felt when his brothers sold him. If a person is hurt or abused by total strangers that is possible to understand, but if cruelty and sadism are perpetrated by one's own brothers, that hurts most; it penetrates and sinks down into the depths of the soul. The blood storms and boils, it does not rest, it is never pacified, as the blood of the prophet Zacharia, which was constantly boiling because he was murdered by his own people.

The brothers realised by now that it was a punishment by the Lord. After careful, thorough self-examination and soul-searching, they arrived at the correct conclusion. They reasoned that after all so many people were coming to Egypt to buy grain. They came in peace and departed without any interferences or accusations. So why were they different to the others? Hence they arrived logically at the ultimate conclusion – "We are guilty". However, Joseph was not fully satisfied with their penitence as it originated from fear and punishment. He would have preferred it that it should result from love and real brotherhood. The brothers reacted with love when Shimon was imprisoned, but Joseph wanted to see what their reaction would be when Benjamin would be imprisoned for theft. Would they also stand up for him, sacrifice their lives and demonstrate their brotherly attachment or would they reject him?

Joseph really rejoiced when he heard their confessions and admission of their guilt. "The Lord has found out the iniquity of thy servants, we are your bondsmen" (44-16). These sincere words stirred in the heart of Joseph a real joy and spiritual satisfaction.

VAYIGASH

Yehuda was the surety for the safety of his brother Benjamin and had promised his father that he would bring him home. Now he cannot return home without Benjamin, so he began to find various ways and means how to convince and soften the heart of Joseph. Yehuda wanted to gauge and understand clearly and with certainty the character of Joseph. Was he a righteous and kind person or a liar, an evil and brutal man?

So he commenced to address him from the humanitarian and mercy point of view. He carefully watched his reactions and replies; he appealed to him to consider his old father and Benjamin who was his darling, whose brother had died.

If he would see that Benjamin was not with them Jacob would die.

Jehuda noticed to his pleasant surprise that whenever he mentioned the name of his father, there was a conspicuous change in Joseph's face, so he decided to repeat the name of his father many times. "For how shall I go up to my father if the lad is not with me, lest I look upon the evil that shall come on my father. Then Joseph could not restrain himself before all of them who stood by him.

He exclaimed: "I am Joseph, is my father still alive?"

There is a question about that verse. After all, the brothers have already told him and assured him that Jacob is alive; why did he ask again? The answer is that by that question he criticised and admonished his brothers. "Is my father alive?" implies that it is not "your father". "Through your brutal action you have repudiated and discarded and renounced your filial attachment. Had you really loved me why did you sell me to the Egyptians? You know very well that our father loved me – so when he would discover what had happened to me he would mourn continually and find no comfort." This actually was the fact; he remained in mourning all the time. "That shows that you do not treat and respect him correctly and dearly as befits his status and position. So therefore he is my father and not yours.

On hearing that, the brothers took fright and moved backwards, fearing revenge and punishment which they deserved, but Joseph reassured them of his good intentions and of his brotherly love and sent them home to bring their father. So he sent his brethren away and they departed and he said to them: "See that you fall not by the way" (45-24).

The Rabbis have commented (Tanit 6) that this advice contains many other recommendations, one being that a person should not walk fast as quick walking affects one's eyesight. By this they meant that when a person wants to embark upon any scheme or undertaking, he has to contemplate beforehand all the pros, and cons., the advantages and the harm which may result. One has to exercise patience and moderation because when a person acts in a hurry, the light of his eyes diminishes, meaning that his thinking and concentration are affected and he will be bound to make mistakes and miscalculations. He neglects his common sense and elementary logic.

That happened when the brothers sold him. They did not think and reason clearly about their cruel action of selling a brother in cold blood. Moreover, by doing so they caused incalculable pain, grief and anguish to their beloved father. All because they were not patient.

Another implied piece of advice was not to interrupt the study of Torah for the study of the Torah saves and protects the person that he should not transgress or overlook any of our religious commandments. The light of the Torah guides and shows him the right path in life.

Finally Joseph said to them to enter a city when it was still light. This was also expressed by Rabbi Yehuda in the name of Rav, as follows: a person should try to depart from a place in goodness and enter under the same circumstances, implying that a person has always to try to look at people and at life at their good qualities and actions – not to sit in judgment over people, neither to accuse them unnecessarily. If one sees another doing or committing a deed which is difficult to comprehend, one should not be hasty or jump to conclusions and find him guilty. One should first try to examine the circumstances and conditions – perhaps he acted under great external or internal pressure. By these words he also implied that his brothers should not have been so hasty in accusing him and selling him.

(45-27) "And they told him all the words of Joseph which he said to them and when he saw the wagons which Joseph had sent to carry him. The spirit of Jacob, their father, revived."

In Hebrew the word for a wagon is Agala which means also a Calf. So our Rabbis have indicated that Joseph reminded him about the sacrifice of a calf. When a murdered person was found between two cities, the nearest city had to bring a calf as a sacrifice. The question is obvious: what is the association? In Deu. 21-1 it is stated that if "one be found slain in the land which the Lord gives you to possess and it is lying in the field, and it is not known what has killed him, then the elders and judges shall come forth and they shall measure unto the cities which are round about him, the slain. Then the elders of the nearest city will bring a sacrifice, a heifer of the herd and they shall speak and say our hands have not shed this blood". The Daat-Zkinim explains why it was necessary for the elders to bring that sacrifice and why they were to blame for that dastardly crime. The commentators said that sometimes the leaders were indirectly to be blamed because they did not prepare the proper schools to study Torah and the people were not given the correct religious education. Consequently, if the correct upbringing of the younger generation is lacking, some become murderers. Because the elders had neglected their duties towards their people, the Torah accused them, as they themselves would have been indirectly responsible.

The same occurred to Jacob. When Joseph began to bring evil tales against his brothers, Jacob warned him against this behaviour, as that might result in jealousy, hatred and even murder. Jacob tried with all his capabilities to teach him and guide him, which is the duty of a parent towards his children because if anything happens to his son, he will be blamed and accused.

The Torah has already mentioned it in the Shma, Deut. (6-7) – "and thou shall teach them diligently while you are sitting in your house" – implying while they are still in your home – "and when you are going in the road" – referring even when they are already adults and are walking on the hard road of life, even then a parent may not dare relax and become complacent in the instruction and teaching of his children. However, Joseph did not take seriously the warnings and admonitions of his father and continued with his evil tales against his brothers. Jacob began to blame himself for his inadequate upbringing of his son as Joseph continued his deplorable and unsatisfactory mode of strange behaviour. Jacob was afraid that he had lost his influence over Joseph, consequently he started to speak to him hard words and taught him the law of the sacrifice of the heifer, hinting that if any tragedy will happen, he, Jacob, will be blamed.

Because of his youth Joseph did not fathom and realise the deep and truthful words of his father. But now after so many years, the wise and justified words of his father caught up with him, at last he understood them. That was the confirmation when he sent the Agolot to his father as if to say: "Now I understand your warning, how right and clever were your words." When he received the confession of his son, Jacob was happy in his heart.

That had confirmed once again that Joseph was still his beloved and pleasant son; he had not made a mistake in the past.

Gen. (46-1): "And Israel took his journey with all that he had and came to Beer Sheba." The Midrash (15) comments: "where did he go?" Said Rav Nachman: "he went to cut down the cedar trees which Abraham, his grandfather, has planted in Beer Sheba and which he had planted in Eishel. When he travelled to a new land to begin a new life, Jacob wanted to build the future of his family on the foundation of his bright and truthful past, on the foundations of faith in the Lord, kindness and honesty which he had learned from his parents and grandfather. Cedar trees are strong and hard; that is the symbol of Judaism. We have to be strong, unwavering and determined in our belief, strong as iron not to deviate and turn from the right path. For the same reason Jehuda preceded Jacob to Goshem in order to establish schools there for learning and synagogues (Rashi). He dispatched Yehuda to prepare appropriate places where his grandchildren would acquire the correct directions and teachings of our Torah.

Our Rabbis (Sanhedrin 15) have already told us that a person is not allowed to dwell in a place where there is no place for teaching the Torah to the young generation. It was a difficult task for Yehuda in a place like Egypt where no places of learning were established before. That was the first condition stipulated by Jacob before coming to settle in Egypt.

VAECHI

"And Jacob lived in the land of Egypt seventeen years." During these seventeen years Joseph supported his father. They were indeed the best years of his life. Emphasising also the great honour and love which Joseph has showered upon his father notwithstanding the fact that being a Viceroy was obligated and very much immersed with government matters, yet he has found time for his father to provide him with all his requirements.

Jacob was also satisfied with the behaviour of his other children. They lived in Goshen in a real Jewish environment which they had constructed. It helped them to guard jealously our spiritual inheritance and not to assimilate among the Egyptians nor to lose their Hebrew identity. "And the time drew near that Israel must die." Jacob had two names, Israel and Jacob. It was already explained by the Orach-Chaim that the name Israel means greatness and glory. In spite of the fact of being in exile, he desired before his death to impress his natural pride and spiritual ascendancy over the Egyptians. He wanted to leave a lasting remembrance for future generations that they should remember him as an independent, free, loving person. He commanded them: "Bury me not, I pray thee, in Egypt, but in Israel in the Double Cave". He preferred Israel over Egypt with all her treasures and riches.

Jacob has by now anticipated that Joseph may ask him why was not his mother, Rachel, buried in the Double Cave but in Bethlehem. So Jacob said: "Rachel died unto me, I still feel the loss of Rachel as I loved her very much. Indeed I wanted to be buried next to her but alas it was the will of the L-rd that her grave should be in Bethlehem". Joseph brought his children to Jacob and he inquired: "Who are these?" (8-9). And Joseph said unto his father: "They are my sons whom G-d hath given me here". And he said: "Bring them I pray thee unto me and I will bless them". The commentators have already remarked that surely Jacob knew his grandchildren! It states later in the verse that he even knew who the older one is. The explanation is as follows: He was very anxious and worried about their spiritual future. Whether or not they will follow him in their belief and religion or will they desert him? Joseph makes a faithful promise: "They are my children and will remain so", but adds: "the L-rd gave me them here, they were born in Egypt, therefore patience has to be exercised but eventually they will return to their Jewish source and root". To this Jacob answered: "Take them to me and I will bless them". It was the duty of Joseph to bring them spiritually to their grandfather, so that the generation gap will be narrowed. Jacob invited his children for the blessing. However, he stipulated by saying: "Gather yourself that I may tell you. Gather yourselves together and hear you sons of Jacob". The prerequisite for blessing is unity. He advises them how to preserve and keep the unity. A stern warning is sounded about the dangerous pitfalls which may destroy and undermine unity. He rebuked Reuben for being unstable and hasty. A person has to be placid, patient and not impulsive. Our Rabbis have said (Shabot 24): Patience is worth four hundred Zuzei (a type of currency)". Haste destroys unity. Simeon and Levi were criticised for not being able to control and contain their anger. Our Rabbis have said (Ndorim 22): A person who becomes angry quickly is like one who worships idols. Anger lies in the lap of a fool. Anger also breaks unity. He praised Juda for his good character which he showed in the case of Tamar when he admitted publicly his guilt to the detriment of his reputation. He blessed Issachar and Zebulun who were partners. While Issachar studied, Zebulun supported him financially. That is real unity. Dan was praised for his trust in the Almighty: "I have waited for thy salvation O L-rd" (49-18). Asher was singled out for his kindness and good heartedness. But Joseph was bestowed with the greatest blessing. Because he forgave his brothers in spite of the fact that they had wronged him. Through that action he showed clearly his excellent character. In that context we may understand the following verses (50 17-18): "And when Joseph's brethren saw that their father was dead they said: Joseph will peradventure hate us'." So they sent a messenger unto Joseph saying: "Thy father did command before he died. Forgive I pray thee now the trespass of your brethren". The commentators have already remarked: when did he say that?

The answer is that when he blessed Joseph as explained above, in the blessing which he bestowed upon him, Joseph forgives them openly and says: "I am going to die, unity has to prevail among us so eventually you will leave Egypt and enter the land of Israel".

SHMOT

"And these are the names"; the sidra starts with a conjunction because the Book of Exodus is a continuation of the Book of Genesis. The Book of Genesis ends with the promise which Joseph assured his brother that they would be redeemed from Egypt. His prophecy was fulfilled and the text gives us the reason for their redemption: "And these are the names", implying that because they did not change their names. Also because they continued the faith of Jacob, they followed in his footsteps. The third reason was they "have striven with all their might and strength to cement and strengthen the unity of the family life", to live peacefully and amicably together.

When the number of the Israelites was small, 70 people,

Pharaoh and his advisers were satisfied with the Hebrews who brought commerce into the land, and developed the country economically and financially. But when the Hebrews increased and multiplied, the Egyptians started to reveal their latent and hidden hatred and immediately took counsel what to do with them. In the beginning they still were ashamed to show their cruelty openly and publicly. However, they carried it out, under the hidden veil of shrewd diplomacy. They imposed taxes, their aim was to demoralise and break the Hebrews economically, although they had also suffered as a result of the unreasonable monetary hardships. The text says "in order to punish him", referring to the Hebrews. The imposition of the severe taxes was done under an excuse – they used the old antisemitic accusation as the Hebrews were engaged in trade they therefore were richer than other sections of the people and as a result had to pay more proportionally. However, their main aim was to oppress and suppress them. When they saw that their scheme failed, as it is written "the more they were oppressed the more they prospered", they embarked on another devilish plan. Pharaoh summoned the midwives secretly and commanded them, "when you will see it is a boy, then you will kill him".

However, it is difficult to understand how he could expect the midwives to carry out his instructions; after all they also were Jewesses. The answer may be because the midwives had changed their Hebrew names, from Yocheved and Miriam to Shifra and Pua, respectively. That change gave Pharaoh the false idea that they had forsaken their people and faith; eventually they would become traitors to their suffering nation and would be instrumental in carrying out his evil plans. Rashi provides a reason for the change of their names; these signify their competence and ability, namely to beautify the children and keep them calm.

The midwives ignored the injunction of Pharaoh. They kept the children alive and, moreover, provided them with the necessary food. Thereafter he embarked on a more obviously destructive plan. All the sons were to be cast into the river. Targum Onkelos adds: "all sons who will be born to the Hebrews". In the text the word "Hebrew" is omitted, so why did the Targum add it? The answer is that in his public decree Pharaoh purposely omitted the word "Hebrew" in order to deceive and mislead general public opinion; that it has nothing to do with the Jews, it is not a racialist law. On the face of it the decree was not directed against any specific section of his people but was a universal law affecting all under his government. This would therefore be an internal matter in which no one had the right to interfere. Secretly, however, he dispatched an amendment which stipulated in detail that it was directed against the Jews only.

In spite of all these inhuman laws, Moses was born and his mother placed him among the reeds by the brink of the river (2-3). This signified the fate of Israel which is continually floating on the stormy and rushing waters of life.

When Moses grew up he went out to his brethren (2-4). Although he grew up at the palace of Pharaoh he did not forget his suffering brothers and their burdens. When he espied an Egyptian smiting a Hebrew, he looked this way and that and when he saw that there was no man there he slew the Egyptian and hid him in the sand (12). Moses was both surprised and angry. Why did the Hebrews allow themselves to be enslaved and subjugated? Who did not resist and rise against their oppressors. Why did they keep silent when they watched one of their brethren being smitten and attacked by an Egyptian? He therefore looked closely at their faces, scrutinised and examined them thoroughly. He wanted to find in them a small spark of pride and resistance. But unfortunately he only saw in them despondency, apathy and weakness. They made peace with their lot and took everything for granted. He therefore had to kill the Egyptian.

The Midrash asks with what did Moses kill the Egyptian? Rabbi Eviatar says "with his fist"; others maintain "with a piece of clay" while the Rabanan say "by mentioning the name of the Lord".

That discussion has to be understood allegorically. The Rabbis were discussing how the redemption of our people will take place.

According to the opinion of Rabbi Eviatar it will be achieved by the fist, implying, we have to stand up against our enemies, to resist and to fight back with vigour and strength, not to humble ourselves at the feet of our enemy. Others maintain through clay, that is to say, by hard work and toil as we see in our land of Israel where our people have returned to our land, toiling on the land as all the normal nations are doing. The Rabanan maintain it was through mentioning of the name of the Lord. But actually it may be said that all the opinions are correct. They complement one another. We have returned to our land through miracles which the Lord has performed for us and helped us, but in addition to that we have had to toil, to cultivate our land and be ready to defend and to fight for our land and for our survival.

On the second day Moses witnessed a heart-breaking incident. He saw how the Hebrews were arguing and he admonished them. They got annoyed, replying insultingly: "who made you a ruler?" Our Rabbis have added that they said insolently, "are you not the son of Yocheved and not the son of Pharaoh's daughter?" Pharaoh was informed of that and Moses was obliged to escape to Midian.

Here Moses pastured the sheep of Yitro in the desert. Targum Onkelos comments as follows: "he led the sheep to beautiful pastures in the desert". What is actually meant by "beautiful pastures"? Moses had purposely led the sheep of Yitro in the desert which is ownerless and where there is no trespassing. The Talmud on Sanhedron 25 states that shepherds were not accepted as witnesses because they used to pasture their flocks in fields which did not belong to them. They were not particular, but in the desert there are no owners and everybody is permitted to pasture. That is the "beautiful pasture"; wherever there is honesty there exists moral and ethical beauty.

When Moses fled from Egypt because his own brethren had denounced him to the Egyptians, he felt a disappointment and grief in his heart. He could not understand the attitude of his own people. They were being oppressed so cruelly by the Egyptians, so why should they denounce, hate and oppress one another? The desperate position in which they found themselves should have united and cemented them together, to live and exist in harmony and unity against their common enemy.

Moses could not find an answer to that burning question. His spirit was confused and despondent. He thought a great deal about the future of Israel and came to a very tragic conclusion. That is why the mountain is named "Chorev", meaning "dry" as it were his hopes, vision and confidence about his own people were at a low ebb, the source of hope had dried up. However, the Lord encouraged him through the scene of the Burning Bush which was burning but was not consumed. That vision represented the future of the people of Israel. In spite of all the difficulties and tribulations they would eventually be redeemed from slavery. According to that explanation we may also understand the words of the prophet Malachi (3-22): "Remember you the Law of Moses my servant which I commanded on him" in chorev for all Israel. Here also the prophet used the word "chorev" and not Sinai. According to the Talmud Malachi is Ezra. He was also in a state of despondency when he witnessed how intermarriage had become prevalent among the higher classes. That was the painful cry to his people to remedy this evil and the verminous deeds which were in a state of dryness, of spiritual bankruptcy and dissolution.

Moses was humble and meek; he did not have sufficient confidence in himself to be the leader who would take them out of bondage. In addition he realised the degrading moral and spiritual state of the Hebrews who were denouncing one another in order to find favour in the eyes of their enemies and oppressors.

Therefore the Lord performed two miracles which were meant to encourage and to strengthen him. The Lord said to him, "what is in your hand?" and he replied "a rod". And He said "cast it on the ground". And he cast it on the ground and it became a serpent and Moses fled from before it. And the Lord said unto Moses: "Put forth thy hand and take it by the tail", and he put forth his hand and laid hold of it and it became a rod in his hand. And the Lord said furthermore unto him: "Put now your hand into your bosom" and when he took it out, behold his hand became leprous, as white as snow – and when he took it out of his bosom, behold it was turned again as his other flesh. In this manner the Lord inducted him into the leadership.

If he puts his hand in the bosom and says everything is finished and lost, there is nothing to do – then the hand becomes leprous, but if in spite of all the difficulties which he may encounter, he still continues his work and actions with vigour and vitality b he does not keep his hand in the bosom, then eventually he will succeed. The important lesson is contained in the diligence and the perseverance with which the aim is pursued.

We may similarly interpret what is said about the rod which is the symbol of leadership. We find people who are venomous and vicious like snakes – blackmailing, denouncing and spreading lies, making derogatory remarks about their leaders, as Datan, Aviram and Korach did. By nature they are cowards and weaklings. The most effective way to subdue and eradicate them is to demonstrate strength and firmness, to show them the rod which will frighten and subdue them. And, indeed, it was so. People denounced and blackmailed him to Pharaoh. However, the Lord has promised him they will eventually be redeemed and released from Egypt and they were neither to waver nor become despondent.

/ *Around the Tents of Torah*

VAEIRA

(6-2) "And G-d spoke to Moses, and said to him, 'I am the L-rd and I appeared to Abraham, to Isaac and to Jacob. But my name I made not known to them'."

The L-rd criticised Moses for not accepting the promise of the redemption of the Israelites from Egypt as the Patriarchs had accepted it with complete faith, and this is indeed difficult to understand. How is it that Moses, the greatest prophet, should hesitate to accept the promise made by the L-rd?

An answer may be given as follows: There is a basic difference between a promise which was made to an individual and one made to a nation. The promise to the Patriarchs was of an individual nature. The L-rd promised Abraham the land of Israel, and yet, when he later needed a piece of land for a grave for his wife, Sarah, he encountered difficulties in acquiring it. Finally he had to pay an exorbitant price for it, yet he did not doubt the words of the L-rd. The lesson of this for every Jew is that one should not lose faith in the L-rd in spite of difficulties and hardships which one may be faced with in life.

Moses's promise was a promise to the nation. The people had unfortunately started to waver and doubted the certainty of their ultimate freedom. The oppression and the misery was so harsh that they could hardly believe in their redemption. Consequently, they began to ask questions. A nation which is desperate and despondent is indeed allowed to ask questions even of the L-rd.

Being the sincere and devoted leader, Moses sided with them and said the following to the L-rd (5-23): "For since I came to Pharaoh to speak in Thy name he had dealt ill with his people, neither has Thou delivered Thy people at all". The nation has already lost its patience and is not able to suffer any more. It cannot tolerate further the dire and bitter state of affairs. That is what actually compelled Moses to ask the impertinent question. However, the L-rd was not really angry with Moses. On the contrary, he likes it, because by this confrontation Moses clearly demonstrated his love for the people, which unequivocally makes him worthy of the leadership.

The above text states "to Abraham, to Isaac and to Jacob". We see that the word "to" is repeated several times. By the repetition the Torah wanted to emphasize that each one of our Patriarchs had recognised the L-rd by his own right and conviction. Indeed, Isaac was helped by his father and he in turn helped his son Jacob. But even without their help each and every one of them would have undoubtedly reached the same conclusion – belief in the Almighty.

"And my name the L-rd I made not known to them." The Yalkut (176) states that for the wicked the name is mentioned first, like "Naval was his name, Sheva Ben Beechri was his name", but for the righteous it is different. There it states – "and his name was Elkana"; "and his name was Boaz", and not "Elkana was his name" or "Boaz was his name". Similarly in this instance, "And my name I did not make known to them".

There is a deep thought in this statement. When a wicked person is doing something noble, there is invariably an ulterior motive. It is done because of publicity and self-aggrandizement; people will speak about him and eventually his name will become known, therefore his name is mentioned immediately. But the righteous person is different. He is an introvert who dislikes publicity and self-advertisement, hence he hides "behind his name".

"These are that Aaron and Moses to whom the L-rd said, bring out the children of Israel from the land of Egypt" (6-26). Rashi remarks that in some places in the Bible Moses is mentioned first while in other places the order is reversed. Rashi gives an answer that demonstrates that both of them were of equal importance. However, another explanation may be added as follows: When

Aaron and Moses came to Pharaoh to plead with him for the redemption of the people, it was Moses who was the spokesman, who knew how to approach the king on an equal level, because he had been brought up and educated in the royal palace as a free person, and was able to mix as an equal with royalty and the other Egyptian dignitaries. Having led a free and dignified life, he had the moral courage to speak to the king fearlessly Indeed he criticised him harshly for taking a free people who had come as guests to the Viceroy Joseph and enslaved them. For that mission Moses was the only right person, and not Aaron who had been born into slavery and lived under oppression. He was, as it were, suffering from an inferiority complex, and did not possess the ability to face up to a king and to speak to him bluntly. Therefore, when it came to approach Pharaoh, Moses had preference and his name is mentioned first. But when it came to approach the Israelites, then Aaron was the ideal spokesman, because they looked upon him as one of them. He had grown up with them, suffered with them and experienced all their tribulations and hardships and, therefore, they trusted him. They looked upon Moses as a stranger who had spent his life in a foreign environment. Secretly some of them may have suspected him as not being sincere. So, when it came to speak to the Israelites Aaron was given preference. His appearance placated and instilled confidence in them.

"And Moses was eighty years old and Aaron eighty-three when they spoke to Pharaoh." The Torah has recorded their age for a specific reason. In our day a person who becomes old is told in polite terms to resign and hand over his position to one who is younger.

Our Rabbis, however, said: "wise, old people, the older they become the wiser they are". (Kanim). That point is clearly demonstrated by Moses. In spite of his old age, he managed to guide our people for more than forty years, energetically and wisely. He commanded the respect even of the younger people.

They did not say mockingly: "What does the old man say or know?" They observed the in junction of our Torah, "Stand up before an old person".

(7-9) "... when Pharaoh will speak to you saying: 'Show a wonder for you'." Actually it should have stated: "show a wonder for me". But that expression contains a bitter sarcasm against Moses, and should be interpreted in this manner: Pharaoh will say this to you: "I maintain that you self-appointed leaders do not believe in your mission. You shout and make a big commotion, but do not believe in what you yourselves preach and demand". He suspected them of being hypocrites. He, therefore, said "show a wonder for you", implying first believe yourself and then try to convince others.

"And Aaron cast his rod and it became a serpent". A snake differs from other animals in that whilst other animals which attack and devour, derive an immediate benefit by satisfying their hunger, a snake kills and harms without any benefit to himself. So it was with Pharaoh. He enslaved and subjugated the Hebrews with harmful results for himself. The sorcerers of Egypt succeeded in doing the same, but Aaron's rod swallowed up their rods, indicating that though Pharaoh might refuse and harden his attitude, in the end he would have to give in. Pharaoh will perforce have to release the Hebrews. The L-rd did not want to punish Pharaoh suddenly without any previous warning and actually showed compassion towards him. Even the wicked deserve consideration. Thus the L-rd says to Moses: "Proceed to Pharaoh in the morning," implying that he should go to him in the morning as long as there was still time, before it was too late, before the twelfth hour had struck. He could still do penance and change his ways, hence the warning. In the beginning Moses did not ask Pharaoh to tell the Hebrews to go, but requested him to allow the Hebrews to go and pray to the L-rd in the desert. This may be explained as follows: first of all Moses desired that

Pharaoh should admit that there is a G-d in the world who guides the destinies of mankind; we are his slaves, and no other person is allowed to enslave his fellow men. Pharaoh immediately rejected the suggestion by saying: "Who is G-d that I should listen to His voice?" Only then, the L-rd decided to bring upon him plagues which would eventually compel him to recognise that there is a L-rd, a high power, who directs and leads the world.

The L-rd purposely chose Egypt as the land in which to show and demonstrate His strong hand through miracles and wonders. The reason may be that had the L-rd revealed His wonders in another place then the other nations could have doubted the existence of the L-rd arguing that Moses had tricked the people of that land who were primitive and uncivilised. But Egypt at that time was already a place of culture and science. They had astrologers, many people of letters and literate leaders. Hence their declaration that there is a L-rd in the world, indeed had a great effect upon the other nations. Consequently, many people came to recognise the existence of G-d.

As Rahav said to the spies whom Joshua had dispatched (2-9): "And she said to the men: 'I know that the L-rd has given you the land and that your terror is fallen upon us and that all the inhabitants of the land melt away before you'." The L-rd had intentionally strengthened the heart of Pharaoh in order to bring upon him more plagues, so through them, the name of the L-rd would become known.

It is obvious that a nation cannot be born in one day. As the prophet Isaiah (vl 66-8) has said: "Is a nation born in one day?" The redemption of a people is a gradual process. In the beginning the L-rd took them out "from under the burdens of the Egyptians" (Ex. 6-6), which indicates that, unfortunately, they had already made peace with their fate, to remain slaves. So the L-rd told them that if they would make a stand to show willpower and demonstrate their resistance, then He would surely help them.

The chance will be given to them to become a civilised and progressive nation who would then be ready to enter the Promised Land. The L-rd spoke to Moses four times, every time using a different expression pertaining to their imminent redemption. For this reason our Rabbis instituted the drinking of four cups of wine during the Seder, corresponding to the four promises. Wine is the symbol of joy and happiness. Happy is the nation which has attained freedom and independence.

BOA

(10-1) "And the L-rd said to Moses, 'Come in to Pharaoh'." The commentators have remarked that it should have stated, "Go to Pharaoh". This may be explained as follows: Moses had already been to Pharaoh several times, but without success because he refused to listen and had abused him. Naturally a person becomes despondent under such circumstances. So the L-rd encouraged him, saying, "Come in", implying that he should enter into the palace, not to be afraid for Pharaoh would eventually take notice of him.

This confrontation with Pharaoh would enable him to tell future generations what the Lord had wrought upon Egypt and the signs and wonders which He brought among them. His going would effect tremendous repercussions upon the future of Israel.

And indeed on that occasion they succeeded in breaking the stubbornness and resistance of Pharaoh.

He said: "Go serve the L-rd G-d, but who are they that shall go?" To that Moses replied: "We will go with our young and with our old". Actually Pharaoh's question is difficult to understand. Here was a nation which was cruelly oppressed and inhumanly trampled down; was it necessary to ask them who would go? They would flee from that accursed place.

The answer is that Pharaoh realised his difficult position, so he granted the Israelites partial freedom. He said: "Go serve your L-rd", so that he might entice them to remain in Egypt rather than to go to the Land of Israel. After all, they had already become accustomed to its climate and to the place, and Israel they had not yet seen. Pharaoh weighed up what course to adopt to placate and win over the Hebrews through deception and false promises. Gradually the Hebrews would forget their past grudges and hatred against the Egyptians and would eventually remain in Egypt. This unfortunately later caused Moses much trouble and worry.

When the Israelites said: "Let us appoint a leader and return to Egypt", Moses immediately replied: "We shall go with our young and old". According to the opinion of Moses, who maintained that all the people would leave Egypt, the young are mentioned first and then the old because the future of every nation depends upon the young and if they are willing to go, the older generation will automatically follow.

Pharaoh was angered by Moses's reply and chased them out. Subsequently the L-rd inflicted upon him more plagues. The Yalkut states that the darkness of the ninth plague was as thick as a golden dinar. By that the Yalkut emphasised an important point, namely, that it is wealth and riches which are the cause of wars and bloodshed, jealousy and hatred. Thus it states (23): "during that period of darkness a man did not see his brother". In life we witness that the rich person sometimes avoids meeting and seeing his poor brother. Therefore the L-rd has commanded: "Speak please now in the ears of the people and let them ask every man of his neighbour and every woman of her neighbour jewels of silver and jewels of gold". By that injunction the L-rd wanted to test the people whether there was unity amongst them. They would not be jealous of one another and therefore they would be able to keep a secret. In a place where there is hatred, the people do not calculate and foresee the dire consequences for all of them. Thus when an enemy will know that his adversary is going to ask for an Egyptian gold vessel, the hatred will blind him to such a degree that he will divulge to the Egyptian that the Hebrew will not return the gold to him, although he himself may also suffer in the process, because he will also fail to get his gold. Thus it was a real test in love and brotherhood which had to prevail among the people. This is the first condition for our very survival. It was the wish of the L-rd that the Hebrews should become rich before their departure from Egypt. The reason is as follows: unfortunately there is a flaw in human nature when a person suddenly becomes wealthy that wealth is sometimes detrimental to him. The money goes to his head; he may lose all human feelings for the poor and needy. Thus the L-rd embarked them upon a gradual and slow process in becoming rich so that when they will enter the land they will already be a people of means and possessions.

"Speak please!" The L-rd had to beg and entreat them to take money. Superficially it is difficult to understand why it was necessary to beg them to take money. People toil in order to obtain wealth and here the L-rd had to beg them to take money. This may be explained in this manner: Whenever a person wants to perform a mitzvah – a good deed – he is invariably opposed by the "evil inclination" which is called in Hebrew "Yetzer-Hara", whose main aim is to create obstacles in his way. This may be proved from the eating of the Paschal sacrifice. The wicked son asks: "What mean you by this service?" Throughout the year the wicked son eats meat and likes it, but when it comes to fulfil the commandment of partaking in the paschal sacrifice, he immediately begins to ask questions. Why is he suddenly reluctant to eat tastefully prepared meat? The answer is that the meat is associated with a mitzvah, therefore Satan appears and tries by means of all kinds of excuses and pretexts to disturb the whole procedure and to mislead. The same also occurred at the Red Sea where money was lying on the ground. They were forced to take the gold and silver.

Thus in Egypt the L-rd had to implore them to ask the Egyptians for treasures because it was a mitzvah and whenever it is connected with mitzvot, the opposition and resistance of the unholy forces is great.

In the same context may also be explained the statement in the Talmud (Bava Kama 87): "In the eyes of the L-rd stands higher in importance a person who was commanded to do it and is doing, than a person who was not commanded to do it and is doing it." This has been explained before. A person who was commanded to do it has opposition from Satan, but a person who was not commanded has no opposition, thus it is easier for him to carry out the commandment than the person who is under obligation to carry out the duties. Thus in the final analysis the injunction to ask for money from the Egyptians was a formative step in the building of the nation.

In this context may also be explained the commandment: "This month belongs to you (12-2)". The L-rd commanded them to count the months of the year. That was also a necessary step in the formation of the nation. They had to remember their past and for that they would have to study when events actually happened. Moreover, they were told to count the days according to our own history and events. It is the duty of every Hebrew to be conversant with our Torah and Prophets. Unfortunately we find that among our youth there are those who know the culture and literature of other nations, but are aware of very little of our own spiritual inheritance. As King Solomon has said in the Song of Songs: "My vineyard I did not look after". That is why the text says: "to you". The events of other nations are not yours, but the events of the Bible are certainly of concern to you.

The injunction about the paschal sacrifice contains a similar thought (12-22): "And you will take a bunch of hyssop and dip it in the blood that is in the basin and strike the lintel and the two side posts". We have to demonstrate openly to the world that we are proud to be Jews and feel honoured to maintain our religion. We do not conceal or hide our Judaism. We reveal it by placing a mezzuza on our side posts. The bunch of hyssop symbolises unity which is imperative and essential for the building of a nation.

The commandments concerning the eating of the paschal sacrifice also contain an important thought appertaining to the redemption of our nation: "and you will eat it in a haste". A nation which returns to its land to build and be built need not live in material luxury. It has to be satisfied with minimum requirements. The main goal is to leave behind exile and dispersion, and the text therefore states: "your shoes on your feet and your stick in your hand". Even if our shoes and sticks be our sole possessions we yet have to rely on the L-rd, who will certainly help us. We have to gird ourselves and proceed with courage and vigour with the help of the L-rd to our Land.

B'SHALACH

"And it was when Pharaoh had let the people go". The Talmud (Megilla 6) states that the expression "Vayehi" – "and it was", denotes a calamity. What kind of a calamity then occurred here? This may be explained as follows:

The actual exodus from Egypt was followed by many tragic events for the people of Israel. When the Israelites wandered in the desert they complained more than once and said: "Let us appoint a leader and return to Egypt". This is indeed difficult to comprehend.

What made them yearn to return to Egypt? Had they forgotten all the cruel deeds perpetrated by the Egyptians against them? It is against common sense for a people to be so willing to return to slavery! The answer is that after realising that he would be forced to let the Israelites go, Pharaoh made a political reversal by misleading and misguiding them to think that he was their friend and protector who let them go because of his generosity and kindness. That was the "calamity", as many started to think that he had freed them willingly, so from that false assumption they started to love and respect Pharaoh and wanted to return to Egypt.

The Lord knew the nature and psychology of the people of Israel, so he did not lead them by the way of the land of the Philistines although that was near, "lest peradventure the people repent when they see war and they return to Egypt". Here we note that the verse refers to the Israelites as People whilst the next verse says "and the children of Israel went unarmed out of the land of Egypt".

The use in the first verse of "the people" and in the other verse "the children of Israel" may be explained according to the rule which is given, by the "Klei" Yakar. Wherever the word "people" – AM – is used it refers to those people who were Egyptians and later became Jews; in other words, Jews of Egyptian origin, but "Bnei Israel" – Children of Israel – refers to born Jews. Now the former, being of Egyptian origin, were responsible for all the upheavals and troubles which caused so much aggravation and unpleasantness to Moses. When the text speaks of returning to Egypt they are "the people" who do not possess a real and convincing belief in our future and in the Lord. They want to live in luxury and comfort so, as soon as they encountered problems and opposition, they changed their minds and nationality as easily as they changed their clothes. But as for the born Jews, they went up armed, ready to fight and if necessary even to die but not to return to Egypt.

(19) "And Moses took the bones of Joseph with him". The Torah here reveals the greatness of Moses. It was indeed a great moment for Moses when the Israelites left Egypt, a time of great rejoicing and happiness. He was the messenger of the Lord who approached them first and told them about their imminent redemption, but the people did not believe him; they wanted to attack and even kill him. He suffered a great deal for them; he had many disappointments and betrayals. They would not believe that he would really free them, so now when his dream was realised he was in a state of spiritual elevation. And yet he was not swept away by the great events of the day; his spiritual equilibrium was maintained. He did not forget the request made by Joseph who had said before his death (Gen. 50-25): "The Lord will surely remember you and you will carry out my bones from him". Joseph was the first one who promised them their eventual freedom from bondage. It was that promise which had strengthened and revitalised their spirit in times of unbearable despondency and pessimism.

According to Rashi, Moses also took along the bones of all the brothers of Joseph. Moses had a profound motive for this. When a nation begins to build a land it has to base itself on its past. He therefore took the bones of all the brothers to remind them that they had not been born slaves but were a people with an important ancestry. That may also be the reason for asking them "and you shall carry up my bones away with you", the expression "with you" denoting it had to be constantly in their minds and hearts, that they originated from righteous and holy people.

Because of that the text states further (21) that: "The Lord went before them by day in a pillar of cloud to lead them the way and by night in a pillar of fire to give them light". The Lord watches over us at all times and periods. In the time of day implying when we are rich and strong we are sometimes tempted to forsake and abandon our religion, and then the Lord leads us back to the right and correct path. And in the night, implying when we are in a state of poverty and oppression the Lord appears to us with his holy light bringing us brightness and cheerfulness, saving us as He did at the Red Sea.

(5) And it was told the King of Egypt that the people were fled and the heart of Pharaoh and of his servants was turned towards the people and they said: "What is this we have done that we have let the Israelites go from serving us?"

Reading the verses superficially it is difficult to understand what happened so suddenly to Pharaoh that he made such an abrupt reversal. That may be due to a psychological reaction. An honest person does not run away in haste, he walks away gently and quietly. However, if he runs away in a hurry he arouses the suspicion of being a thief who has committed an evil act and is endeavouring to escape punishment and retribution. Pharaoh was concerned when he was told that the Israelites had fled and that the whole story about their freedom was treacherous and false, he felt misled and tricked, therefore he decided to chase them.

The Yalkut (230) advances the following reason – "they said because of them we had prosperity in the land". This is characteristic of the Jew-baiters in many lands. They oppress and degrade the Jews in their midst but nonetheless are reluctant to let them free. They need the Jews to cover up their mistakes, to use them as a scapegoat. If there are hunger, famine or any crisis in the land the blame falls upon the Jews. In spite of the fact that our people are discriminated against, yet the way to their freedom is barred and closed.

When the Israelites saw the Egyptians pursuing them they started to complain to Moses (11): "And they said to Moses: 'Because there were no graves in Egypt you have taken us away to die in the wilderness'."

The Yalkut (232) relates that four parties were formed by the Israelites – one maintained "let us fall in the sea"; others said "let us return to Egypt"; the third group shouted "let us wage war"; the last one declared "let us pray fervently to the Lord". Those parties are still in existence today! There are Jews who have unfortunately lost their faith and therefore in time of despair either commit suicide or assimilate. "Let us fall in the sea" means into the sea of assimilation and oblivion. To that party Moses replied in his song: "I will sing to the Lord for He is highly exalted. The horse and his rider has he thrown into the sea". We have to believe in the eventual help of the Lord which arrives swiftly.

Those who wanted to return to slavery he rebuked by saying: "Till thy people pass over we are slaves to the Lord and not slaves to slaves". To those who wanted to wage war he exclaimed: "The Lord is a man of war". But to those who suggested "let us pray to the Lord" he said: "The Lord shall reign for ever". This is the real faith in the Lord.

In that context we can understand the holy words of the Yalkut (238) interpreting the verse (14-29): "But the children of Israel walked upon dry land in the midst of the sea and the waters were a wall unto them on their right hand and on their left". "On their right hand" refers to the Torah while "to their left" refers to the Tephillin, meaning that we were redeemed from slavery because of our pure confidence and reliance on the Lord. Subsequently Moses was stirred to render a song to the Lord because of the manifestation of their belief in the Lord. "And they believed in the Lord and in his servant Moses".

Then Moses sang a song of thankfulness, "the Lord is my strength and song". The "strength" refers to the Torah (Yalkut 244). Our national and spiritual strength is the Torah which gives us courage and vitality to survive. The same happened afterwards when they arrived at Mara. They could not drink from the water for they were bitter, so they murmured against Moses saying

"What sail we drink?" and the Lord showed him a tree and he cast it in the waters and the waters were made sweet.

Rabbi Eliezer Hamodee says it was an olive tree which has a bitter taste. A miracle occurred, that out from the bitterness resulted sweetness. There is a deep thought in this statement. We are commanded to give charity but people sometimes complain, asking why we should diminish our possessions by parting with some of our money; we should rather abstain from giving donations so that our wealth will accumulate. Some rationalise their desecration of the Shabbat by quoting the well-known saying that "time is money". We should rather work an extra day to increase our fortunes. The Lord therefore has demonstrated that out of our presumed bitterness and poverty, sweetness will result. On the contrary, we will be wealthier and happier by giving charity, by observing Shabbat and all the other commandments which we were told to observe.

In that context we may understand the next verse (25): "There he made for them a statute and ordinance and there he proved them."

Rashi comments: In Mara the Lord gave them some of the commandments such as Shabbat. The Lord tests us with the observance of Shabbat. Unfortunately there are some people who cannot stand up to that test, they succumb and weaken for the sound of gold. But the miracle of Mara may serve as an historical example – namely the Lord will compensate and repay our presumed losses. We also see that in the miracle of the Manna (16-5): "And it shall come to pass on the sixth day that they shall prepare that which they bring in and it shall be twice as much as they gather daily". On the sixth day they gathered a double portion of manna for Friday and Shabbat. That was to serve as an example for posterity that the Lord will provide sustenance and food for all those who observe Shabbat.

Thus when the Israelites started to murmur, the Lord punished them. Amalek came out to attack them. (17): "And Moses said to Joshua: 'choose for us people to wage war with Amalek'." The reason for choosing Joshua to be the commander-in-chief in that particular battle, is given in the Talmud: Joshua was a descendant of the tribe of Joseph!

There is a profound meaning to this. Amalek attacked us without any reason or cause; we did nothing to him, we were too far from his boundaries to constitute a threat to him. The main cause was our belief in the Lord, as the text states that "a war between the Lord and Amalek in every generation". The hatred of Esau to Jacob is neither rational nor logical, it is a venomous hatred.

When he was Viceroy of Egypt Joseph had the experience of saving the Egyptians from starvation and hunger. And what was his reward and appreciation? Hatred and jealousy, followed by slavery and murder. Therefore Moses chose Joshua. Being a descendant of Joseph, Joshua had certainly been told of the history of Joseph which would encourage him to fight with great determination against our historical enemy. This was so, "and Joshua weakened Amolek and his nation by the sword".

YITRO

Yitro has been given the signal honour and privilege of having a Sidra of the Bible named after him, and a very important one which is the account of the receiving of the Torah. The reason why that honour was bestowed upon him is mainly that he had also accepted Judaism unconditionally and convincingly – an act that was, as it were, his own receiving of the ten commandments.

He had also advised Moses how to organise effective order in the leadership of people. This advice was gladly accepted and carried out by Moses and contributed to strengthening and preserving unity and harmony among the people. It follows therefore that a person who was instrumental in bringing about such harmony deserved an important reward, which was the naming of a Sidra after him.

(1) "And Yitro heard": Rashi asks what was it that he heard? The two great events were the cleavage of the Red Sea and the victory over Amalek. These two are of course basically different. At the cleavage of the Red Sea the Israelites were a frightened and impotent people; they had contributed very little towards the annihilation of the Egyptians. Everything was done for them by the Lord, as the text states: "Speak to the people of Israel and let them proceed". In the war with Amalek, however, they were neither flurried, nervous nor frightened. They fought heroically, calmly and in an orderly manner and won.

Examining and analysing their achievements Yitro arrived at an important and surprising conclusion: the people of Israel were unique. Overnight, as it were, they had been transferred from a nation of slaves into a well organised and strong fighting army who could stand up against the might of Amalek. They were led by their young leader Joshua who belonged to the new generation and this augured well for the future of the People of Israel.

"The priest of Midian, Moses's father-in-law". Why the repetition? It is already known that he was the priest of Midian. Here the Bible emphasizes the greatness of Jethro who, although a priest of the idols-worshipping Midianetes, amongst whom he had attained a high position, yet accepted Judaism with deep joy. He was therefore fit and suitable to be Moses's father-in-law. According to our Rabbis penitence reaches up to greatest heights even to the presence of the Lord (Yuma 86).

Verse (6) states: "And he said unto Moses, I, thy father-in-law Jethro am coming unto thee". We notice that here the text does not mention the fact that he was a priest, for already that belonged to the past and now he was proud that he was the father-in-law of Moses only.

(8-9) " ... and Moses told his father-in-law all that the Lord had done to Pharaoh ... " And Jethro rejoiced in the Talmud. There is a difference of opinion as to whether Jethro really rejoiced sincerely or only superficially. It is difficult to understand these two opinions which are diametrically apposed to each other. It may be said however that one opinion complemented the other. Indeed, Jethro felt both joy and pain. Firstly when Moses told him about the exodus of the Israelites with all the miracles which accompanied them, together with the goodness which the Lord has done to Israel, he was happy and rejoiced, for Jethro had been one of the ministers in Pharaoh's cabinet who had resigned and fled when Pharaoh embarked upon the killing of innocent children. He wholeheartedly opposed cruelty and injustice and sincerely he never agreed to what Pharaoh did. But when Moses told him about the plagues, punishments and plight of the Egyptians he was filled with an instinctive grief and pain.

(10) "And said Jethro, blessed is the Lord who saved you". The Yalkut comments (268) that Rabbi Papus said it was an insult to Moses and to the Israelites who had not blessed the Lord until Jethro started the blessing. It is a difficult statement to understand; had not Moses rendered a song to the Lord?

But we may approach it from a different angle. Certainly Moses and the Israelites had blessed the Lord; but they were obliged to express their appreciation and thankfulness to the Lord for the freedom which had been given them, for the miracles which had been performed when they were saved from certain death. However, when Jethro blessed the Lord it was not for miracles in which he had been personally involved. It was really an unselfish act on his part. It was a genuine blessing. In that instant Jethro has excelled himself. Before the receiving of the Torah Moses had, through the clever advice of Jethro, organised an effective judicial system to keep order and preserve justice among the people. These are amongst the fundamentals of our faith upon which our Torah is based; without justice and fairness our religion has no basis. The Yalkut (280) quotes Rish-Lakish as saying that the Torah which was given to Moses was written with black fire on parchment of white fire. The white fire is the symbol of blessing and success. When we carry out and observe the commandments, then the Lord blesses us with an abundance of goodness and prosperity; however, if we deviate from the correct and proper way then we are confronted with the black fire, which is the symbol of the curses contained in the Admonition.

That may also be the reason why the Lord has appeared to us in a thick cloud. (19) "I come unto thee in a thick cloud – accompanied with thunder and lightning". He warns the Israelites that should they become unruly and inattentive then clouds and punishments will descend upon them, and accordingly tells them to "take heed yourselves that you go not up into the mount or to touch the border of it, whosoever touches the mount shall be surely put to death". This was a hint that we are not allowed either to criticise, change, add or subtract any injunction or word of the Torah as that may result in spiritual suicide. Therefore the Lord said: "and prepare and sanctify them today and tomorrow". Holiness needs preparation; a person does not become a holy man overnight; hard work, exertion and diligence are required for this.

The Israelites received the Torah and exclaimed: "We shall do and listen" – they would carry out the precepts of the Torah before listening and understanding. They realised at once that the Torah is fathomless, very difficult to know and comprehend. They therefore immediately expressed their confidence in the Lord, promising that they would observe the commandments blindly, without even understanding them. This would come later by fulfilling and practising the commandments. Moses, however, tried his utmost to explain the reasons of the commandments to them. (5) " ... And Moses went down to the people and said to them". The expression "and he went down" may be explained as "he descended to their level of knowledge".

Moses certainly knew all the secrets and hidden meanings of the Torah but when he spoke to them he went down from his elevated spiritual heights and taught them according to their standard of culture which was simple and uncomplicated, in order that they might grasp and understand easily. The Ten Commandments were written in a clear style; they are concise and to the point so that the people should never say that they did not understand and thus find a pretext for the sins which they might commit.

This may also explain the reason why the ten commandments were written in the singular. It was the explicit desire of the Lord that every individual should understand everything clearly, for in the eyes of the Lord every Jewish person is considered equally important. (Bara Batra (10).) The Talmud tells us that in the beginning the Lord offered the Torah to Esau and Ishmael, but when they refused, the Torah was then proposed to the Israelites and they immediately accepted.

At first glance it is difficult to understand why the Torah was not offered in the first place to us. There was, however, a special reason for this. Had the whole of humanity accepted the Torah then we would have enjoyed freedom, peace and prosperity. The first Temple was destroyed because we worshipped idols, as some of our people were influenced by other nations who had done so for many years. We imitated them as some of us wanted to be as other nations. Also many of our people had been persecuted by the descendants of Esau and Ishmael for religious reasons, but if all of them would have worshipped and believed in the same religion, then we would have lived in harmony, tranquillity and peace.

(22) "And if thou make me an altar of stone thou shalt not build it of hewn stones for if thou lift up thy tool upon it thou hast profaned it".

Here we have the basic difference between Judaism and other religions. Whereas peoples of other beliefs have compelled other nations and communities to accept their various religions, we are forbidden to do so. Moreover if a non-Jew wants to accept Judaism we have to discourage him by telling him (Yevamot) that we are the constant victims of unending persecution. Naomi similarly discouraged Ruth by telling her what disadvantages and sufferings she would have to endure by becoming a Jewess.

Generally speaking, we are not allowed to pride ourselves on our strength. King David whose ambition in life it was to build the holy temple, was forbidden by the Lord to do so (Chronicles 1-21) – "You won't build a house to my name because you spilled too much blood". Other nations honour those who gain victories at the cost of numerous innocent lives. We, however, were commanded not to use iron for the construction of the altar. Rabbi Shiman, the son of Eliezer, comments: the altar was given in order to lengthen the years of a person, the iron shortens the longevity of a human being, therefore we are not allowed to lift the object which shortens the years of an object which lengthens it. The Lord purposely forbade us immediately after the receiving of the Torah to enforce our religion upon other people. We are quite satisfied that the Hebrews should remain faithful to their religion without trying to coerce other people to become Jews.

(23) "Neither shall they go up by steps unto mine altar"; here the Torah has commanded us not to become arrogant about our religion. We have to live in peace and unity with all people.

MISHPATIM

(21) "Now these are the ordinances which thou shalt set before them". The same was repeated in (Deut. 31): "And teach thou the children of Israel, put it in their mouths".

Immediately after the receiving of the Torah the Lord commanded Moses that he should revise it constantly with the Israelites until they would know it thoroughly and clearly; this was essential to enable them to understand how to carry out the commandments. Our Rabbis (Avot 6) stated that "An ignorant man cannot be a sin-fearing man". In a similar manner the great Rabbi Akiva advised the teachers to revise their subjects frequently with the students (Yalkut 301). Rabbi Akiva himself affords an example. He had been a shepherd but eventually attained the great heights of culture through diligence and scholarly revision of his studies.

The first commandment he taught them concerned a Hebrew slave. If a Jew stole and on being caught has no money to compensate the owner for the articles which the latter has lost, our law is opposed to sending the thief to jail. Experience has shown that the jail is invariably the place where the first offender is thoroughly trained in crime, our ancients decided on a different course of action. He was sold as a slave but one who had nevertheless to be treated with consideration and even respect.

The Rabbis stated (Kiddushim 22): "Whoever buys a Hebrew slave, he buys a master for himself". The Yerushalmi adds: "If the owner possesses one cushion only he has to give it to the slave and the owner must sleep on the ground". The late Gaon Rabbi Chaim of Volozhin, of blessed memory, logically explained that if the owner possessed one cushion only and yet owned a slave, it was only to boast about it to the neighbours; an act of snobbery as it were. Such a one had to be discouraged from such an empty and stupid attitude and therefore he had to bear the consequences. We may infer from this what are the real qualities of freedom and human dignity. Even a thief has to be respected and actually helped in whichever way possible because man was created in the image of the Lord. Most of our laws are based on this basic principle. There has to be a positive and friendly relationship with one another; we must beware lest we cause damage or loss to our neighbours; we must respect their persons and possessions and render aid if necessary.

"If fire breaks out and catches in thorns so that the shocks of corn or the standing corn is burned". Our sages explained this verse allegorically as follows: said Rabbi Shimon, the son of Nachmoni: the wicked people cause all the upheavals in the world but it begins from the righteous. He compared the wicked to the thorns and the corn to the righteous.

The statement is difficult to understand. Perhaps it may be explained as follows: in the history of our People we have experienced how arguments and friction were started among the righteous – as between the chasidim and mitnagdim for example – which caused deep wounds among our people with lamentable historical repercussions. These sad events are very difficult to explain. The only feasible explanation which may be advanced is perhaps the one that the environment and frustrating conditions in which they were living were the cause of them. Indeed, they were surrounded by "thorns and snakes" which had a detrimental effect upon them, with results that were harmful and deplorable.

Our sages have added another interpretation (5): "The person who makes the fire will pay compensation, said the Lord". "I made that Zion should be consumed by fire and I will rebuild it by fire". This may be explained as follows:

Our Rabbis narrated in Gittin that the second Temple was destroyed because of inner hatred for the sake of hating only. Jealousy and hatred are a hidden and dangerous fire which destroys and consumes everything which may oppose and resist. It can destroy lands and even continents. The fire of hatred has destroyed Zion. But the evil was created by the Lord, as Gen. states: "At the entrance the sin is in lying so the Lord accepts the responsibility for the results of hatred. However, the Lord will erect a wall of protecting fire: the effects of hatred will be eliminated. Then fire will bring light and cheerfulness to humanity".

One of the causes of jealousy is when the capitalist whom the Lord has blessed with wealth looks arrogantly and abusively at his poor brother, refusing selfishly to help and support him; thus we were told to support the poor.

(22-30) "And you will be holy men unto Me, therefore you will not eat any flesh that is torn of beasts in the field (treif) you will cast it to the dogs". Commentators have already remarked about the association between being holy and giving certain things to the dog.

The "Daat Zkinem" provides the following interpretation: we hope to show our appreciation to the dog for risking his life while defending our herds from being devoured by wild animals. Our faith is based upon the principle of appreciation, so we have to thank the Lord for sustaining us. Similarly we have to honour our prophets for the same reason. Our Rabbis (Avada Zara 5) have already elaborated on this subject. The prophet Isaiah (1-3) exclaimed angrily: "The ox knows his owner and the ass his master's crib, but Israel does not know, my people do not consider". In our holiness even the dog has to be appreciated, let alone human beings. The Lord will certainly reward us.

"And you will serve the Lord and He will bless your bread and your water (23-25)". The verse in Hebrew starts in the plural and ends in the singular, a point on which the commentators have already remarked. The following explanation may be given: To serve the Lord we need a religious environment because subconsciously and instinctively the individual is influenced by the spiritual climate in which he lives. If one dwells among the righteous then the individual is also similarly affected. Our Rabbis, therefore, advised us (Ethics 10) to dwell among learned and intellectual people. The text therefore enjoins us to worship the Lord in the plural. However, when it comes to food the tastes differ and vary, depending upon the individual person as also on the place and climate; it is, therefore, written in the singular.

"And I will remove sickness from the midst of you" (10) may be explained in a lighter vein. There is a sickness which a person is sometimes ashamed to relate. For example, A bought a house cheaply and sold it for a profit. However, after the sale the value rose. Inwardly he is upset but he cannot divulge that to others as they would ridicule him and say: "Why complain, you had your profit, why be greedy?" So the Torah assured us that even complaints like these the Lord will remove from the midst of you.

(24-1) "And to Moses the Lord said, 'Ascend to me'." According to the Orach-Chaim, that took place after the receiving of the Torah. After the people of Israel had exclaimed "we shall do and listen", they were in a state of spiritual elevation. Moses was also elevated to great spiritual heights. The leader and his people are intertwined for there is no leader without a people.

Indeed that was the aim of Moses during his lifetime – to teach and strengthen his people in faith and religion. And he sent the young men of the children of Israel who offered burnt offerings and sacrificed peace offerings, etc. Moses emphasized here that our future depends entirely upon the youth. If they will remain faithful to Judaism, even to be prepared to bring sacrifices for our religion then our religious and national future is assured.

(12) "And the Lord said to Moses: 'Come up to me into the Mount and be there'." The expression "be there" underlines the following advice to scholars: We sometimes witness that students who have attended school for many years do not make the desired

progress. More often than not they are to blame for they have not applied themselves to their studies diligently. They did not pay the required attention to their teachers. Physically they are in the classroom but their thoughts and wishes are in other places. Therefore God asked him to "Be there", your thoughts should be concentrated on what he would learn.

"And I will give you tablets made of stone". There may be a reason why the tablets were made of stone. The composition of a stone consists of many particles of sand, concentrated in one place, cemented by various chemicals which transforms it into a mighty element. The same principle was applied to study. A person does not become a scholar overnight; one has to study continuously and diligently, gather and absorb knowledge gradually. Such efforts will eventually be crowned with success. That is the only way to succeed and achieve progress in the study of the Torah: to concentrate and gather all the wisdom into one channel of belief and faith which will cement the knowledge for eternity.

TRUMA

The sidra of Mishpatim instructs us in the ways of justice, honesty and righteousness, followed by the injunction to practise charity and philanthropy. Indeed, charity is an important mitzva, but the money has to be honest money, earned in a decent and dignified manner, not by deceit or robbery. The prophet Isaiah in chap. 1-12 speaks bitterly against these vile practices – "Who hath required this at your hand to trample my courts, your hands are full of blood". Therefore it was emphasized that they take it for me, saying: "If you know that everything is in order then you may take their contribution". It states that they take and not give; to admonish the collectors that they may not take charity if they knew that it came from an undignified source. The reason is the that the Lord said: "they will erect a ... sanctuary that I may rest in the midst of them". If the sanctuary is erected then through dishonesty, bribery and illegitimate means, how can we expect the divine presence to be there? Our Rabbis have already indicated that (Bara-Batra 81): "Charity is so important that it brings nearer the coming of Messiah", meaning that the coming of Messiah depends upon prevailing and conducive elements of justice and truth. These are the imperative conditions before the revelation of the divine.

For in a place of evil and robbery holiness and brotherly love cannot be accommodated. Similarly says the Prophet (Isaiah 10-3) about the coming of Messiah: "And he shall not judge after the sight of his eyes, etc., but with righteousness shall he judge the poor and decide with equity for the meek of the land", meaning that the Messiah will not lavish compliments and praise on each and every good-hearted Jew, but will first investigate thoroughly the source of the money.

(3) "And this is the money offering which you will take from them": According to our sages that money offering was supposed to act as a forgiveness for the sin of the golden calf. It may be interpreted thus: in life we find that when a person becomes affluent he makes his money his idol, which he worships. He begins to measure values and ideas in life by means of a material yardstick. If a venture is financially profitable then it is worthwhile getting involved in it. However, if a matter is of spiritual significance only, then they refer to it sarcastically, as being a matter for dreamers and impractical people.

In heaven the angels start asking questions: Why should a person of that calibre be endowed with wealth? Had he remained poor, perhaps his religion would have been enhanced. To silence all these heavenly critics, the wealthy person demonstrates that the money with which the Lord has blessed him is positively and helpfully spent and distributed, by saving people from starvation and the giving of charity. This acts as an atonement for the golden calf.

And they will make an ark of shittimwood which is according to the Talmud (Bara Batra 80). A tree which even after being cut down is regenerated from its roots. It may be called the tree of life, meaning that, although the tree is cut down there is still a future for it for a new and vigorous stem will grow from the root. This is what actually happened to our people more than once. The tree of our people was cut down and destroyed by our vicious enemies. Many Jewish communities were uprooted and scattered across the globe yet in spite of all the difficulties which they have encountered they succeeded in establishing Torah and Jewish centres, because the roots of our nation were sound and grew again. And where did Moses acquire the Shittim wood? The Midrash (B'reshit Raba 33) explains that before his death Jacob commanded his children to prepare now the wood for the Lord would order them in the future to build a Temple. Even when the Israelites are in Galut they are to be constantly aware of the inevitable building of a Holy Temple. The tabernacle in the desert was of a temporary nature, indicating that even while we are being driven from pillar to post we still have to establish some sort of temporary spiritual and religious centre whence the light of our Torah and faith will emanate. History has borne this out.

In the Galut we established Yeshevot, Torah centres, which kept the lights of our Torah burning. The Midrash (33 Breshit) gives this reason why the Ark was constructed before the other vessels. Just as at the creation of the world the light was created before – "And the Lord said let there be light" – similarly in the Temple the Torah is also called light, therefore the Ark preceded all the other vessels.

From that our Rabbis have learned that the importance of a Synagogue depends not upon the exterior construction of the building, the decorations, the furnishings, which are also necessary, but rather upon the spiritual beauty, meaning the study of Torah, the observance of Shabbat, and the spreading of Judaism among the youth which is the main pivot of our faith.

"And you will make two cherubim of gold (25-18)": Rashi comments they had faces of a child, implying that young children are as pure as angels, honest and sincere, ignorant of flattery. They are direct and faithful to our Torah. The danger begins to become apparent when they approach adulthood. Then some start to deviate and revolt against tradition and teachers, therefore the most auspicious time to educate them is while they are young and pure.

(25-18) " ... of beaten work shalt thou make them at the two ends of the Arkcover." Jewish education has to be linked inseparably with the holiness of the Ark. We have to make our children mindful of the sanctity of the Ark and the Tablets which are placed there, and instil a desire to guard them jealously and lovingly. It was hammered out of one piece of gold, implying that faith and religion result eventually in unity and brotherhood.

(25-22) "And I will speak with thee from above the Ark cover, from between the two cherubim which are upon the Ark of the testimony", implying that the presence of the Lord will rest in the midst of you through the continuation of our faith by the youth which will ensure eternity of the Torah.

(25-31) "And thou shalt make a candlestick of pure gold, of beaten work shall the candlestick be made, its cups, its knobs and its flowers shall be of one piece with it". The candlestick (Menora) is the symbol of our faith as the believer of the Lord carries within him a pure and joyful light which brightens and cheers up his road in life. But it has to be of one piece, reminding us that there may not be any contradiction between the Synagogue and the home. We find that while some of our co-religionists are in the Synagogue they make promises that they will observe the commandments and ask forgiveness for their sins. On coming home they forget all their promises and continue as before. Thus our Torah has said "of one piece" implying that there may not be any contradictions between synagogue and home. All the commandments have to be fulfilled, those between man and man as well as between man and the Lord. The flowers of the Menorah indicate that our Torah is not old, she is always in a state of blossoming freshness and newness.

(25-40) "And see that thou make them after their pattern which is being shown thee in the Mount". Our Rabbis stated that the Lord showed him a Menorah of fire teaching us that the study of Torah has to be performed with warmth, enthusiasm and sincerity.

In the Yalkut (369) Rabbi Yishmael states that three laws were difficult for Moses to grasp until the Lord had explained them to him by example. They were Menorah, Rosh Chodesh (beginning of the month) and which animals we are allowed to eat.

That Yalkut may be explained allegorically – Moses could hardly understand how it is possible to bring a synthesis between the home and the synagogue, as that is one of the most difficult tasks. The Lord, therefore, advised him that if commandments will be carried out with honesty and self-sacrifice then the rest will follow in an orderly fashion – that is the Menorah of one piece.

In the birth of moon we witness that after a period of darkness the moon is reborn again spreading light over the horizon, driving away the shadows of darkness. This is symptomatic of what happened to our people after periods of oppression, holocaust and near-annihilation. We have appeared again in our land. In that we see the guidance of the Lord who promised us that we shall exist forever.

T'TSAVE

(27-20) "And you will command the people of Israel". Many commentators have remarked about the change in the style of expression. The name of Moses is not mentioned; the text says simply – And you will command. It could have stated it thus: and the Lord has spoken to Moses and you will command. The explanation may be as follows: It was the first command which Moses conveyed to the people. It is in human nature that power corrupts, therefore the Lord uses "You" to emphasize that you were also created from dust and will return to dust, therefore be humble and considerate in your approach to the people; remain patient, kind and understanding with them. Moses indeed retained his humility throughout his lifetime even under the most difficult circumstances.

"And they will take to you pure olive oil". The Yalkut (375) comments that it had to be bought with public money. The light of the oil lamp is the symbol of the Torah which scatters and drives away darkness, evil and wickedness. For that we need the participation of the whole nation. The dove also brought an olive leaf in her mouth to Noah but it was of little significance, as immediately after the flood the people reverted to their mischief and sin. One person cannot achieve much in face of determined opposition; the whole people, therefore, were asked to contribute.

The oil had to be pure and clean, to emphasize that our intentions and thoughts have to be pure and honest.

"Beaten oil for the light": there is a sad fact in our history that whenever we are oppressed and downtrodden, we are creative, spreading the light of Torah to the world. It was in Babylonia in exile that the great Talmud was compiled; and the reverse is also true: when the sun of affluence shines upon us, we tend to neglect and even to rise against our religion. Thus we were told to light the candles of Torah in all times, from evening to morning. In

Rabbi N. L. Marcus

that sense we may understand what our Rabbis said about king Hezekiah (Brachot 4): After the defeat of Sennachrib's armies around Jerusalem, the king offered a prayer of thanks (King 1120-3): "And have done that which is good in thy sights", refers to the fact that he attributed his victory to prayer. That was a great virtue in Hezekia; normally, when a person becomes popular and mighty he prefers to boast about his own ingenuity, wisdom and superiority. However Hezekia attributes all his successes to the Lord, which shows the goodness and greatness of his character.

(27-21) "The light was burning in the tent of meeting without the veil which is before the testimony". The light of the Torah has to illuminate and penetrate into the outside world, meaning that the observance of the Torah has to be performed and carried out with so much enthusiasm and warmth, that its influence and presence should be felt among all the sections of the nation. In the same sense may also be explained the verses of Samuel (1-13): "And he opened the doors of the Lord". It refers to Samuel who opened the doors of the Temple so that its holiness would guide and teach the outside people. The sanctity of the Temple may not be confined to the four walls of the Temple only. It may not remain in a small corner but the living waters of the eternal well have to spread and penetrate everywhere; to clear away all wickedness and impurity. A similar story is related about the Vilner Gaon. He studied in his house with shutters closed but his influence and holiness had an enormous effect upon society.

(28-1) "And bring thou near unto thee Aaron thy brother". According to the commentators Aaron apparently was not pleased to assume any kind of leadership as he had witnessed the problems, aggravations and disappointments which Moses had experienced. He was timid and humble, a peaceful and home-loving person.

The great Rabbi Yehoshua, the son of Prachai, has said (M'Nochot 109): "Whoever will suggest to me to assume leadership I will bind him and throw before the lions". However, when one is appointed he may not decline as we see in the case of Moses. At the beginning he was not very enthusiastic about his appointment as a leader, nevertheless he assumed leadership upon the insistence of the Lord.

(28-2) "And you will make holy garments for Aaron your brother, for splendour and beauty". In conformity with his high position and his important standing among the people, Aaron had to dress properly and even impressively. However, it is not the garments which honour the person, it is rather the person who brings honour to the clothes he wears. A person who is suited to a high position is worthy of his appointment so he may be said to bring splendour and glory to those who have appointed him.

(28-12) "And you will put the two stones upon the shoulder pieces of the ephod – And Aaron shall bear their names before the Lord upon his two shoulders for a memorial". On the stones were engraved the names of all the tribes. Intellectually the tribes were not equal, as may be seen from the fact that even Jacob and Moses divided them into categories, but as a leader Aaron may not show any favouritism or bias to the educated, rich or strong. He had to carry them upon his shoulders. That will be glory and splendour of Aaron.

(28-55) "And it shall be upon Aaron to minister and the sound thereof shall be heard when he opens into the holy place before the Lord". The Lord advised him that if he wished to serve the people sincerely and honestly, then his voice, opinion and guidance would be accepted and respected, because invariably Jews respect a saint and honest person. However it is not easy to become a saint overnight. For that one requires preparation and education, therefore the Lord commanded Moses that Aaron had to be initiated and inducted by sacrifices, signifying that a real leader has to be prepared to bring sacrifices. Similarly that was the real test of Isaac being prepared to be brought as a sacrifice.

(29-20) "And you will give (the blood of the sacrifice) upon the top of the right ear, upon the thumb of their right hand and upon the great toe of their right foot".

A leader needs three qualifications in order to succeed. He needs an ear to listen to all complaints and murmuring criticism and must try to rectify them. Our Rabbis (Ktubot 5) had an interesting remark about the tip of the ear. They asked: "Why is the ear hard and the tip soft?" When a person hears something unsuitable, like slander or gossip, one has to place the tip into the ear – he should not accept immediately the slanders prior to investigation and scrutiny. Therefore the Lord criticised King David for he accepted the gossip of Tsiva against M'fiboshet, without finding out the correct position and circumstances. A leader must also be prepared to go from place to place and even from house to house to make peace between people, and to collect funds for the necessary institutions, for our Rabbis have stated that "where there is no meal, there is no Torah (Ethics 3-21)". This is a reference to the toe of the right foot. Moreover the leader must also make his contribution, the strenuous toil of collecting does not absolve him from the mitzvah, "you shall open your hand" (Deut. 15-8). He may not tarry or waver by giving pretexts. Aaron has to serve as an example to Jewish leaders of all time.

KEE-TISAA

(30-12) "When thou takest the sum of the children of Israel": There are various interpretations about the word "Keetisaa". The Midrash interprets it as meaning payment. The Israelites have not paid their debt for their sin of the golden calf. It is a shame to avoid payment but if the debt is settled then everything is eventually forgotten. Therefore the Torah described firstly the settlement and then the sin. The sin itself is one of the most difficult subjects to comprehend. How is it possible for a nation after receiving the Torah, witnessing the greatness of the Lord and exclaiming "we shall do and listen" to make a stupid reversal in a short time and make an idol? Our Rabbis have tried their utmost to delve into their mentality and way of thinking. They have suggested various reasons for this strange behaviour and attitude.

The (Midrash 41) states the opinion of the Rabanan thus: Satan had deceived them with an illusion. He had made them see how Moses was hanging in the air – between heaven and earth, so that the people indicated with their fingers saying: "This is Moses the Man".

In each generation Satan appears in various forms and images trying his utmost to mislead, as Zechariah (3-1) mentions "And Satan standing at his right hand to accuse him", he appears in the disguise of a person to criticise and find fault with our Torah. He thus causes anarchy, disunity and commotion, and under these circumstances his mission becomes easy to accomplish. It is favourable ground for him. The Satanic intentions and schemes are put into action. Actually they deny the existence of the Lord.

But they did it diplomatically. They argued that Moses was not a human being as he hung between heaven and earth, meaning that he did not grasp the problems of ordinary people; he stood higher than life itself. That argument convinced them. But the Torah is not suitable for ordinary human beings, it is rather suited for angels and heavenly bodies.

(32-1) "And when the people saw that Moses delayed to come down from the Mount". Our Rabbis have commented that Moses was delayed by six hours, implying that Moses was behind the times, his teachings were suited to the old generation when they were slaves, but now they were free, on the way to build a land and attain independence. At such a time there was a need for a new culture which would be suited for the new land. The Israelites therefore made a golden calf. And why a calf? King David in Psalm (106-20) says: 'Tor the likeness of an ox that eats the grass". When we examine the psychology of the people who worshipped idols we see that whatever has served them beneficially and faithfully is worshipped and respected by them. Various trees which caused rainfall, the sun, moon and other heavenly bodies were likewise on their lists of idols. Similarly was the ox, which was used for ploughing, riding and also for meat. So they made a graven image of it and danced around it. According to the Talmud the non-Jews have said the Jews wrote down upon the horn of the ox, that you denounce your Lord, implying you have to worship an entity which serves you economically and materially.

About Moses they spread rumours. According to the Yenatan Ben Uziel, Moses was consumed by his holy fire – which belongs rather to heaven and not to the earth.

(32-6) "And they rose up early on the morrow and offered burnt offerings and the people sat down to eat and to drink and rose up to make merry". Rashi interprets "making merry" as referring to immorality. The Yalkut adds (391) "there was also bloodshed". Here the Rabbis give us an insight into the aims of the children of Israel for making the golden calf. Actually deep in their hearts they wanted to practise immorality and bloodshed, but were afraid for the punishment which would follow. So they have established a new faith according to their wild temptation. They preached that religion had to be subdued and guided by their temptation modified and reformed in accordance with times and place. All their evil deeds were committed under the guise of religion which gave them, as it were, a kosher stamp. In our times we also witness that some of our brothers are also misguided by the same cry: We shall dictate religion but not to be dictated to by it! This eventually results in assimilation and disintegration.

After the Israelites had received the Torah Exod. (29-11) states: "And they did eat and drink", whereas after the sin of the golden calf it states: "And the people sat to eat and drink". Food is important but unfortunately there are people who live to eat, their whole existence revolves around eating, and that is what happened at the golden calf – they sat to eat, implying primacy, it was their main aim in life. It is also written in the future tense, indicating that after finishing their meal they already started to worry about the next meal. However, when receiving the Torah, "sat" is mentioned. "They ate and drank" is written in the past tense, conveying the impression they ate, but afterwards they did not dwell upon the importance of that. ...

It is told about the "Chofetz-Chaim" that once during a meal he remarked that the fish is tasty but then added with regret: "what have I to do with the fish?" and stopped eating.

(32-7) "And the Lord spoke unto Moses 'go get down'." Our Rabbis added (Brachot 32) that the Lord told him: "Go down from your greatness; I granted you greatness because of them only". That was a personal rebuke to Moses. When a disciple of a great man deviates from the path of decency, we are inclined to criticise the teacher. We may say that his way of teaching was not suitable, exertion on his part was lacking. Thus the Lord said (8): "They turned aside quickly out of the way which I have commanded them". In an indirect manner Moses was responsible: not long before they had received the Torah when they had witnessed the most profound miracles, so no one would have expected to make such a sudden reversal to worship the golden calf with such enthusiasm and joy, without any regret and appreciation for the past. That was an indictment against Moses. "Your nation was corrupted" thunders the Lord, "you took them out of Egypt, you risked your life and now see what has happened". Naturally that was a great insult to Moses, so the Lord begged Moses (10):

"Now therefore let me alone, that my wrath may be kindled against them and that I may consume them". By this perhaps the Lord asked Moses that he should forgive them for his shame and embarrassment, then He the Lord would forgive them all for their sins against Him.

So immediately (11): "And Moses besought the Lord". Moses forgave them without any hesitation for causing him insult and degradation.

As a prerequisite for their forgiveness, the Lord asked them that every person should give a half shekel. Our Rabbis add that the Lord exhibited a burning half a shekel to him. The reason for that special fiery demonstration was to convey to the Israelites that charity has to be given with warmth, good heartedness and genuine kindness, without any ulterior motives and selfishness.

Why a half only? The reason is that the way of penitence is very difficult. However, our Rabbis have assured us that when a person reveals a sincere inclination to be cleansed then the Lord will help him. So the sinner has to accomplish a half only, the other half will be contributed by the Lord. Therefore the Lord told them to give a half shekel only, and He would help them with the rest of their endeavour to rectify their sins.

"The words were engraved on the tablets". In Hebrew the word for engraved is "Chorut", which also means Freedom, implying that a believer is a free person, he is not a slave to his own temptations and wickedness, he is able to overcome and avoid all the obstacles and pitfalls of life. He has control over his deeds and actions. When it pastures, an animal may eat even poisonous grass, as it is directed by compulsion and instinct. We were told to avoid certain foods however tasty and tempting they may look and smell. It is forbidden, therefore you have to abstain – that is freedom of action and thought. Similarly, Rabbi N'chuma Ben Hakana said (Ethics, Chap. 3-6): "But who that breaks off from him the yoke of the Torah, upon him will be laid the yoke of the kingdom and the yoke of worldly care", meaning that he becomes a slave to himself, eventually becoming powerless to free himself from his own sinful ropes which were created by him.

Moses succeeded by his prayer in obtaining forgiveness from the Lord for their sin of the golden calf. He ascends again to heaven to receive the second tablets.

When he descended his face sent forth beams and they were afraid to come near him. (34-40) The obvious question is why did his face not send out beams the first time when he ascended to heaven? The answer may be that after the people had exchanged Moses for a calf it became necessary to impress everybody with his greatness, whereas the first time Moses, being humble, had refused special honours accorded to him as unnecessary. This is in accordance with a statement made by Rabbi Eliezer (Sanhedrin 52): At the first meeting between an Am Haaratz (Ignoramus) and a Talmid Chaddam (Talmudical Scholar) the latter is treated like a golden vessel, then he depreciates gradually to silver and finally to clay, as familiarity breeds contempt, so it was imperative that Moses should make a great impression upon the people by means of something unusual.

In Yalkut 40-7 Rabbi Yehuda, the son of Nachman, states: The reason for the beams which came from his face is that whenever he wrote something of the Torah inevitably some ink was left in his pen. That may be explained symbolically that the greatness of Moses was contained in his meekness; even after he revised and studied, he still felt that there was still more to know and to study, more ink has remained to write more about the Torah and our religious science and culture.

VAYAKHEL

(35-1) "And Moses assembled all the congregation of the children of Israel and said to them". After the death of the three thousand people as a result of the golden calf, Moses suspected that perhaps secretly, animosity and resentment prevailed against him, so he made a test whether the people still respected and cherished him. Consequently he invited them to a meeting to see how they would react.

The result was favourable. They came and he told them: "These are words which the Lord has commanded, that you should do them", thus underlining an important point that the future of Judaism is based upon deeds and not upon words and speeches only.

Unfortunately we witness this phenomenon in our time. At bar mitzvah celebrations many speeches and promises are made and yet our synagogues remain empty. Thus he warned them: "You have all been at Mount Sinai," and exclaimed "we shall do and listen and yet not long after that great experience a golden calf was made". The reason for that spiritual failure was that while you were at Mount Sinai, you were busy and occupied with making speeches and sermons and you forgot the whole purpose of your presence at that spot". So Moses emphasised that practical deeds and useful results speak louder than flowery and eloquent speeches.

Moses also mentioned the building of a holy Temple, but added that the importance of the place was not to be confined to the exterior beauty, the expensive stones, bricks, carpets and golden ornaments. These may be necessary but their significance would be in the holiness, devotion and the holy spirit which would have to be paramount. A body must have a soul otherwise it remains an empty shell. Thus he told them about the observance of Shabbat.

The observance of Shabbat is, as it were, the thermometer of Judaism. In those communities where Shabbat is observed correctly, there Judaism has a future. It will flourish and will eventually become deeply and strongly rooted. But on the other hand, in those places where the Shabbat is desecrated and abused, there unfortunately the future for Judaism is not so bright for the foundation is missing, so the very structure may sink. Bearing this in mind it is possible to explain what our Rabbis have stated and which is also mentioned in Rashi, that the building of the Temple was forbidden on Shabbat because the holiness of the Shabbat stands higher in importance than the building of a holy Temple. Our people can exist without a holy Temple but will not survive without the observance of Shabbat.

After they had been enlightened about the importance of Shabbat, Moses asked for their contribution for the building of the Mishkan (Holy Temple) which had to be given voluntarily, so he said: "Take from you". It was also a test whether they were satisfied with his leadership as well as a test of their character. As our Rabbis have stated in Eiruvin 65 – the nature of a person can be tested in the following ways: his pocket, in his drinking habits and in time of anger.

That they all passed the test is witnessed by the verse – (20): "And all the congregation of the children of Israel departed from the presence of Moses". He added another important injunction. (35-10) "And let every wise-hearted man among you come and make all that the Lord has commanded".

The giving of charity is very important; however, the collector and organiser stands higher in esteem in our tradition.

Our Rabbis have already mentioned that (Bava-Batra) the organiser and collector of charity stands higher in importance than the contributor. The reason is explained that whereas the contributor is tested once only, while giving, the collector experiences many tests of insults and embarrassments. (35-22) "And they came, both men and women".

The reason why women are also mentioned here is that in Bava Metzia 87 Rabbi Isaac said that women are sometimes reluctant with charity, therefore the women also came along in order to make the giving of charity more difficult and thus the reward will be greater. In spite of the presence of the women who may not be so enthusiastic about giving charity the hearts of the men were not affected.

(29) "Every man and woman whose heart made them willing to bring for all the work which the Lord had commanded by the hand of Moses to be made". Here "for all the work" is emphasized because there are contributors who are willing to donate for the most holy and important objects in the Temple or Synagogue only, to be displayed in the most conspicuous places, where their names should be engraved in golden letters for everyone to see. The text points out that the givers did not stipulate where their money should be spent; their charity was genuine and sincere.

The workmen and architects were also honest and devoted people. They have constructed and worked with faithfulness and deep love.

(36-1) "And Bezael and Oholiab worked all the work for the service of the sanctuary". It has already been remarked that the verse uses the past tense although they had not as yet started the construction. Moses had already invited them to do the work – that may be explained that this refers to the preparation of the work. Before starting work the architects have planned and experimented for themselves ceaselessly to utter perfection in order to accomplish the construction faultlessly. Similarly the expression (36-4) "Game every man from work which they wrought" – the Yalkut comments: his work he did and not the work of his friend.

This may be interpreted in two ways: Firstly, each architect was an expert in his profession, specially trained for that purpose only.

From that we may gauge how much importance Moses attached to the building of the sanctuary, that he entrusted it to experts and famous people only.

Secondly, that there existed a spirit of unity, they lived amicably together, there was no jealousy, each one minded his own work.

(3) "And they brought it to him, freewill offerings every morning". The word "morning" is repeated to emphasize that charity should be given while a person is still young and strong. He should not say: "When I will be old then I will give". The word "morning" refers to youth; one should give when one is still young and vigorous. One should also remain in the state of youthfulness, without getting tired quickly of giving. What our Rabbis have told us in Bava Metzia: "You have to give and give even a hundred times", may be explained to mean that if one has to give charity it is sometimes better to divide it in hundredth parts to give to as many poor people as possible and not to give to one only.

P'KUDEI

(38-21) "Here are the accounts of the tabernacles even the tabernacle of the testimony as they were rendered according to the commandments of Moses". Rashi remarks on the fact that the word "tabernacle" is repeated thrice in this verse. This is so as it refers in addition to the two Temples which were destroyed.

Actually why this place was chosen for a reference to the destruction of the Temples may be explained as follows: Our Rabbis (Talmud) have mentioned the reason for giving "an account to the people" because there were actually some people who suspected Moses of embezzlement of the funds which he had collected. They accused him of gambling and stealing. That in itself was evil and very degrading. That Moses, the greatest prophet of all, who sacrificed his life for the welfare and future of the Israelites, should reap such abuse and insults! Yet the fact is there, however deplorable and hurtful it may be; we had a low-class element among us.

Generations later the destruction of the temples was also caused by slander, hatred and jealousy. Prophets too were stoned, attacked and even assassinated. So, by the asking from Moses for a detailed account because they suspected him of dishonesty, they sowed the seeds of discord, animosity and destruction of the future. That is why the expression "for an account" used here has two meanings – account and reminder. This may be interpreted as: I forgive you now but in the future I will hold you responsible even for the past. It is like a suspended sentence. When gold, diamonds and other valuables were collected for the creation of the golden calf no one dared to ask for an account; on the contrary, all were overjoyed and exuberant when the calf appeared. However, at the construction of the Temple questions and doubts were expressed. Basically that is the difference between holiness and profanity. Where it concerns goodness and sanctity then Satan appears in various shapes to destroy and sabotage all endeavours at creating and promoting holiness. However, when it comes to constructing evil and wickedness, then Satan changes his tune, trying with all his skill and slyness to help, encourage and abet. However, with the building of the Temple the Lord overlooked and forgave them for their past sins.

(39-32) "Thus was finished all the work of the tabernacles of the tent of meeting and the children of Israel did accordingly to all that the Lord commanded Moses, so did they". Although everything was done and accomplished by Moses, yet all the praise and honour was lavished upon the people. For the Israelites it was indeed a great achievement. Considering their sin of the golden calf it was a great spiritual advancement, an enormous stride in their faith. After all the petty complaints, protests and trouble-making, of asking accounts and balance sheets they erected holy Temples and for that spiritual progress alone they deserved an accolade.

Moreover, after 210 years of slavery, participation in holy work is indeed a great achievement.

Later in verse 43 Moses expresses once again his appreciation. "And Moses saw all the work and behold they had done it as the Lord had commanded even so had they done it and Moses blessed them". Moses had scrutinised and examined all the work of the building and expressed his admiration and appreciation for their perfect craftmanship. His part in the achievement he modestly omitted to mention. He blessed them with these words: "May the presence of the Lord rest in all your activities", meaning that just as you have carried out and accomplished something great because you listened to the Lord, so should you act in the future, with sincerity for the real glory of the Lord and our Torah. You will also be crowned with the same success.

The commentators have already remarked about the following contradiction. Verse 40-1 states "on the first day of the first month you will rear up the tent of the meeting" whereas verse 17 reads "and the tent of the meeting was secured up", implying that it was reared up by itself. The explanation may be as follows: Indeed the Lord commanded Moses to erect the Temple, but when the Lord realised the difficulties and problems which Moses encountered, the vicious opposition which had arisen, He helped him in the actual erection of the Temple.

(40-32) "For the cloud of the Lord was upon the tabernacle by day and there was fire therein by night, in the sight of all the houses of Israel throughout all their journeys". With this verse we finish the Book of Exodus. Each of the five books of Moses contains a theme: that of Exodus is the building of a nation. In this book we are told how the people of Israel became a nation, rising from slavery into freedom.

The last verse conveys to us this successful achievement and its reason. No other nation has suffered so much and experienced so many upheavals as we did, but in spite of it all we survived and remained spiritually intact. Although we lived in darkness, surrounded by many clouds of oppression and savagery, we never abandoned our belief in the Lord. There was the "fire" of the Lord even in the night; in the darkest hour of our history it was faith in the Lord which sustained us. In all our wanderings, when fate has scattered and thrown us away, even here the presence of the Lord is there. That is our spiritual strength and might.

VAYIKRA (*Leviticus*)

"And the Lord called unto Moses and spoke unto him". Here is a change in the normal style of the Bible which had invariably started with "And the Lord has spoken unto Moses". We may explain it in this manner: After he had done so much for the Israelites, freed them from slavery, brought them to Mount Sinai and built the Mishkan, Moses might have thought in his humbleness that his mission had been completed. His elder brother, Aaron, would have the task of initiating the young Kohanim so Moses prepared himself to retire and live quietly. The Lord, therefore, called him in order to awaken him as it were from his retirement and urged and encouraged him to do his duty. His work was not yet terminated; more specifically he was chosen to teach them the duties and the laws pertaining to the sacrifices.

The verse starts with the burnt offering which is consumed completely. That sacrifice is supposed to forgive atheistic thoughts and agnostic inclinations. For a person with such convictions it is most difficult of course to adjust to a religious life. It is much easier for a person who had committed sins because of temptation to do penitence than for a person who transgressed the commandments out of atheism. Moses, however, had overcome all the obstacles, had elevated himself to great spiritual heights and returned to his religious sources; for that he deserved a special honour, so he was mentioned first.

(1-3) "He will bring the offering of his free will". A sacrifice has to be brought voluntarily for the whole principle of bringing the sacrifices has to be done with full conviction. It is a matter between him and the Lord who knows all our thoughts and actions, thus before coming to the Temple one has to cleanse oneself from all spiritual impurities and evils.

Rashi adds that the Lord has told Moses to ask the Israelites whether they would be willing to bring sacrifices. Why especially in regard to sacrifices were they consulted first? The answer is that sacrifice is one of the most difficult subjects to understand. There are many queries and finer points which are difficult to grasp. Great belief in the Almighty is required for this, therefore the Lord enquired whether they are ready for these commandments.

(3) "When any man from your people will bring a sacrifice": The Hebrew version starts in the singular and finishes in the plural. Herein is a relevant idea: Our religion has always required sacrifices from us. These were started by individuals like the biblical Nachshon who jumped into the Red Sea, a heroic deed that influenced the others to follow suit. That is why, in the matter of sacrifices, the verse starts in the singular and finishes in the plural; the single individual shows the road and others then follow him.

(1-11) "And shall kill it on the side of the altar northward before the Lord". What reason can there be for specifying the North? We maintain that if a Hebrew has sinned it is because he was lowered into a dark place, he was in unfavourable circumstances, perhaps resulting from wealth or temptation. That sacrifice has to be brought on the northward side as the sun never appears in the north, it is constantly dark. Spiritual darkness misleads a person into doing evil.

(2-1) "And when any one bringeth a meal offering unto the Lord, his offering shall be of fine flour". That applies to a poor man who cannot afford to bring cattle and is given a chance to substitute it with flour which, however, has to be fine and clean, implying that the sacrifice has to be brought with clean intentions.

The procedure was to take a handful of flour and burn it on the altar, then the remainder was allowed to be eaten. This may be interpreted that human nature makes it difficult for a person to part with his possessions for which he had toiled, so the Torah commanded us otherwise: "Give to the Lord whatever you have in your hand, so the remainder will remain with you". It is a kind of assurance.

(2-4) "No meal offering shall be made with leaven, nor any honey". This can be explained symbolically. Self-love and self justification are inseparable parts of human nature. Even the greatest sinner may find excuses and pretexts for his mistakes and failures, so when a person decides to do penance he should not tarry or postpone it; he may not leave it as it were to become leaven or sour for he may change his mind. He should act swiftly upon his resolve to become a better person.

Money is the symbol of sin; in the beginning it seems so sweet and pleasant as King Solomon depicts (Proverbs).

(2-13) "And every meal offering of thine shalt thou season with salt". One possible reason for this is that salt retains the heat, implying that the same spiritual warmth and enthusiasm which had prevailed during the time of bringing the sacrifice while he was in the sanctuary, should remain with him even later when he comes home, where he has to face the most difficult problems. His holy decisions should not be altered in spite of all the obstacles which may crop up.

(4-3) "If the anointed priest shall sin so as to bring guilt on the people" may be explained allegorically. Experience has proved that sometimes when a leader makes a blunder or even a small mistake, there is an immediate outcry against him; accusation and vicious criticism are directed at him. Even Moses could not escape it; they even accused him of adultery! Very few want to grant him the benefit of the doubt. However, when it concerns the sin of the individual, the attitude changes, people speak of goodwill and of forgiveness. So the Torah points out that on many occasions when the leader commits a sin, the people should take the blame upon themselves for they are the cause of it. They either did not provide their leaders with a decent standard of living or they did not respect him as befitted his position. Our Rabbis have already said "do not judge your friend until you will be in his position". The Torah, therefore, writes "the guilt on the people", implying the people have to take the guilt upon themselves. The anointed had to bring an ox – a large sacrifice. When an important person committed a sin its effects were more harmful than a sin of a humble person: he had to bring an expensive sacrifice.

The priest had to bring the sacrifice himself to show that he repented of his sin; that in itself was part of his penance.

(22-7) "When a ruler sinneth he has also to bring a sacrifice". Our Rabbis have remarked "happy is the generation when a leader brings a sacrifice". Why the happiness? The explanation may be given as follows: A leader who is doing nothing will not make mistakes but will also achieve nothing, as he sits with folded arms. However, if he makes mistakes it proves at least that he was active. It was already said that "there is no righteous man upon earth who is doing good and sinneth not", implying that if a person acts he is bound to sin as no person is infallible in his deeds.

TSAV

(6-2) "And the Lord spoke unto Moses saying 'command Aaron and his sons to bring a burnt offering'." Rashi remarks that such a special command entailed diligence and perseverance. Many commentators have already asked why it was necessary to give them a special warning to Aaron concerning the burnt offering. The Yalkut (6) maintains that the burnt offering was supposed to forgive the sin of the golden calf.

The teachers of ethics expounded that a person does not spontaneously become a big sinner; he does not suddenly commit major sins; it is rather a gradual process. Firstly, he commits minor sins and then gradually undertakes major sins and serious crimes. Similarly the Israelites did not become idol-worshippers of the golden calf immediately; it was rather a gradual process.

In the beginning they committed minor sins, followed afterwards by major transgressions until it culminated in the heinous crime of the golden calf, which to them was a great achievement as it is recorded that they jumped and rejoiced with it.

Our teachers have compared spiritual sickness to bodily sickness. Just as it is advisable for a sick person to seek immediate medical attention, as delay may be most serious. So when a person feels some spiritual defect, if his belief weakens for example, or he finds some uncertainty in his faith, he should not tarry but should approach the right authority for advice and help. Rabbi Pinchas, the son of Yaiv, said (Avoda Zara 20) – "diligence and quickness caused cleansing of sin", meaning that when a person feels that his belief is beset by some spiritual malady, he has to act swiftly. Therefore after the sin of the golden calf they were told to be diligent in their service to the Lord. Rashi adds that the priests had no benefit from the burnt offering as the whole sacrifice was consumed. They were reminded not to mind their loss but rather concentrate on their holy work. That may be explained symbolically. When asked why they do not observe various commandments, some people immediately reply: because they can hardly afford it. They have no time for they need all their time to attend to their business. To them "time is money" and they cannot spare the time for their religious obligations. The Torah therefore corrected us, saying: "do not be misled by false ideas and conceptions. The fact is that the Lord repays for the time devoted to religious purposes; you will not suffer any loss, on thee contrary, you will still benefit from it".

(6-2) "This is the law of the burnt offering". The Yalkut states that the Lord said this for the present time as well, even when there is no temple. Now we are unable to bring sacrifices but the study of the Torah takes their place; and indeed it is a sacrifice. When a person closes his business and straight away runs to pray and to study – that is a sacrifice! His friends may mock and laugh at him, but he does not take any notice of them and proceeds on his way to serve the Lord with joy and trepidation.

In the Diaspora when life was hard and unpleasant, that was our sacrifice – the study of the Torah!

(6-2) "It is that which goes up on its firewood upon the altar all night unto the morning".

Night is the symbol of oppression but the sun will eventually rise to bring light and success. It will be caused by devoted study of the Torah.

In the text the beginning of the word "firewood" is written in small type to denote that righteousness and prayer have to be executed and accomplished in humbleness and modesty. Neither in storm nor in thunder does the Lord appear, rather in the soft spoken word. One Rabbi has remarked that a pious Jew sometimes runs so quickly to do a mitzva that in his rush and anxiety he may insult and knock over a friend!

SHEMINI

(9-1) And it came to pass on the eighth day that Moses called Aaron and his sons: There is a rule that whenever the text states "and it came to pass" it denotes tragedy (Megila 10). Indeed there was a tragedy, the sudden death of Aaron's two sons Nadav and Avihu. Aaron felt guilty for their deaths. He had been appointed high priest and the Lord punishes an important person more severely than an ordinary one – "them that are near Me I will be sanctified (10-3)". He was also punished by being forbidden to enter the land. In this regard the Lord is very particular with the righteous to the minutest detail. So, when the crown of priesthood was given to Aaron he was sad and unhappy. He was afraid of the punishment which might follow; and it turned out to be the death of his two sons. And another reason was that Aaron had brought a special sacrifice to atone for his part in the making of the golden calf, for he was a humble person and maintained that he was solely responsible for the calamity which had subsequently occurred. Now he realised that perhaps he had to make a stronger stand against the instigators of the diabolical plan. He was now ashamed and despondent about his past action. He could not face the people, and that was indeed a tragedy for him. His joy turned into mourning. Moreover, Moses comforted him, saying: "Come near to the Altar". According to Rashi he said that seeing that Aaron was ashamed that in itself was his forgiveness. If a person feels embarrassment for his evil deeds that reveals his sincere repentance.

Aaron was a true believer in the Lord. Even when struck by a great tragedy he kept still and did not complain; he accepted the judgment of the Lord in complete faith. The greatness of a person is revealed during the period of his adversity and trouble.

(9-6) And Moses said: "This is the thing which the Lord commanded that you should do": The Yalkut (9) states that

Moses said to the people of Israel: "Remove the evil spirit from your heart then you will all be unified for the service of the Lord". The same as He is one, so should your service to him be one.

In the day of Aaron's induction Moses advised him that the secret of success depended upon his service to the Lord. Invariably he has to remember the Lord. As King David said: "I always placed the Lord before me".

(7) "And Moses said to Aaron: 'Draw near to the altar and offer your sin offering and your burnt offering and make atonement for yourself and for the people'."

Moses inducted Aaron in his holy service, advising him how to be a successful and acceptable leader. It is for the leader to show an example, to practise what he preaches. He has to be the first to bring his sacrifice for the people and his faith; then the people will follow him faithfully and devotedly.

The Yalkut (523) states: the priests had blessed the people after they had acknowledged publicly their unconditional faith in the Lord; meaning that the priest who blesses the congregation has to possess a convincing belief in the Lord so that his benedictions will indeed be of effect.

(9-23) "And Moses and Aaron went into the tent of meeting and came out and blessed the people". The verse is written in the singular, and Moses is mentioned here first. This emphasizes the greatness of Aaron who, although senior in years, yet honoured and respected Moses, as a pupil is supposed to respect the teacher. Hence it is written in the singular to demonstrate the unity and real brotherhood which existed between them.

(9-24) "And there came forth fire from before the Lord and consumed upon the altar the burnt offering and the fat, and when all the people saw it they shouted". They did not praise the Lord but shouted without any respect or honour, and this probably resulted in the tragedy of the deaths of Nadav and Avihu. (10-2)

"And there came forth fire from before the Lord and devoured them and they died before the Lord".

Our Rabbis have advanced various reasons for their untimely deaths. Some say they had shown disrespect for their teachers by expressing opinions in front of them when not asked to do so. Others maintain the reason was that they asked how long the old people would still live. When they would all die, they – Nadav and Avihu – would show everybody how to guide the people.

According to the "Evan-Ezra" they did not use the holy fire but took their own fire. That actually sums up their guilt; they became arrogant. Convinced of their own superiority, they did not use the holy fire, or the teachings of the Lord. They embarked upon preaching and spreading their own gospel; of reforming and modifying the Torah; therefore they have shown disrespect to Moses and Aaron for they maintained that their knowledge was second to none. Consequently that led them to say "till when will the old people still be alive?", which is indeed a horrible question.

For Aaron it was a tragic occurrence and a great test of his belief. In the moment of his greatest joy he was overwhelmed with grief and mourning but he did not complain; "and Aaron held his peace". The Baal-Haturim compares it to the sun which stood still and kept the peace at the command of Yehoshua at the battle of Givon.

The sun carried out the command of the Lord without any question although it was against nature. Similarly Aaron also acted against human nature; he subdued his paternal feelings and emotions. Apparently that was also part of his induction. Afterwards he was told "drink no wine nor strong drink". Normally a person is allowed a small amount of alcohol, but not a leader. He has to abstain from some types of food which are even permitted to others; he has to be the exception; because he teaches and directs others he has to be different. He has to know how to differentiate between the holy and profane. A mistake by a leader may cause hardships and harm to many others.

TAZRIA

(1-12) "And the Lord spoke unto Moses: If a woman be delivered and bear a male child ... The Yalkut (547) states that Rabbi Simloee said that just as the creation of Adam followed the creation of the animals, so were laws of cleanliness, concerning animals, promulgated firstly and then those of man. The reason why man was created last is explained thus: The Lord had prepared everything before the arrival of Adam in order that he should be able to enjoy all the types of food and drink. He was like a guest at a wedding; before the guests arrive everything is carefully prepared for them beforehand.

Everything was created for man. He might have said that, seeing that he was so important he could, therefore, eat everything; nothing was prohibited. Therefore the Lord said that man may not act like an animal which has no control over temptation and appetites. A person has to abstain from foods which are harmful spiritually and which may have a bad effect upon his health.

"She shall be unclean seven days" (Nida 31). The disciples of Rabbi Simon have asked him why a woman who had given birth to a child had to bring sacrifice? He gave them the following answer: while delivering the baby her pains are so enormous that she makes an oath not to become pregnant again. However later she changes her mind so the sacrifice is supposed to forgive her for her broken promise.

From that we can gather the fickleness of a human being and the difficult circumstances under which he is living and existing. We all know the obvious purpose of marriage; however, while going through the labour of giving birth, she is sorry for herself and makes hasty promises, which, immediately after giving birth, are broken. From that we can learn how unfathomable and inexplicable is the mind of a person. King David has said (Psalm 116): "All men are liars". In Simchat our Rabbis have stated: "Look upon a person whom you do not know as a gangster".

(3-12) "And in the eighth day the flesh of his foreskin shall be circumcised". The Yalkut narrates that the wicked Tarnusnurus once asked Rabbi Akiva why a child is not born circumcised seeing that the Lord wants circumcision. To that Rabbi Akiva replied: "The Lord gave us commandments in order to criticise ourselves" – this answer contains one of the basic thoughts of our faith.

The Lord enjoined commandments on us by means of which we should cleanse ourselves spiritually. The fulfilment of them is an education in our upbringing and tests us how far and deep is our belief. Circumcision is a case in point. There have been many opponents, even from our own midst, who have opposed it on the grounds of cruelty and primitiveness. However, today even gentiles practise it for health reasons.

Indeed all our commandments have valid reasons for their fulfilments but these were purposely omitted. Had they been written down some of the people might have said that these reasons did not apply to them. This point is proved in the Torah. There are two commandments for which reasons were given but they unfortunately misled King Solomon precisely because of them. Deut. (16-18) speaks about a King – that he should not multiply horses to himself, nor cause the people to return to Egypt. Neither should he multiply wives to himself, that his heart turn not away. So here the reasons were stated categorically for not having many horses and wives. But King Solomon maintained that these laws did not apply to him, for, being a wise person, they could not affect him. Unfortunately we know now that it ruined him and our people. Perhaps, had the reasons not been stated King Solomon would not have taken the liberty of disregarding the warnings. This is one of the reasons that no reasons are given for the commandments.

(13-2) "When a man shall have in the skin of his flesh a rising or a scab ... " There seems to be an association between the laws which are related to women at the time of their impurity and leprosy. It was medically established that the children might be afflicted with various sicknesses – if the proper laws were not observed during the time of the impurity of the woman. The Torah did not divulge the reason as it seems to be superfluous, just as it is not necessary to give a reason why a person may not eat poison. The contact with a woman during the time of her impurity is also dangerous physically and spiritually.

Rav Ashi says in the Yalkut (551): An arrogant person will eventually be punished with leprosy. The reason may be as follows: Normally atheists are arrogant people who advance opinions about the creation and the existence of the Lord which are beyond them. However they think that they are superior and more clever than others. So they ignore the commandments; they keep on saying: "We are modern and advanced people and do not belong to the old generation". The Lord may punish them, measure for measure. They boasted and became arrogant; eventually they will be confined outside the camp which is the place for lepers. That will bring them to humility. Although the leper may have been a sinner, yet the attitude of the Priest had to be friendly and encouraging. The priest had to come and attend to him. Our Rabbis said (Sifro, Chap. 3) that the priest is not allowed to examine the lepers on a cloudy day or during twilight as he would not be able to see well. That may be explained allegorically. Although he was a sinner yet the priest had to look at the bright side of his personality: it may have been due to circumstances and conditions beyond his control. The Rabbis (Ethics 1-6) have said: "Judge all men in the scale of merit".

METZORA

(14-2) "This shall be the law of the leper". According to our Rabbis (Ktubot) a person was punished with leprosy because he had spoken evil and slandered his friend behind his back. It is measure for measure; he desired through his slandering and falsehood to exclude his friend from society, to ostracise and leave him outside the camp, therefore he was punished with an infectious sickness which shut him out from society.

Our Rabbis asked if this is so, why are we not punished accordingly; many of us frequently commit the sin of slandering. The answer our Rabbis give us is that morally we are on the decline. The previous generation was compared to angels, whilst we are mere human beings; but if the former generations were like human beings then we are like asses. It is well known that on an expensive and fine garment the smallest stain is visible; this ruins it; but on a sack or coarse cloth the defect is slight. The same principle may also be applied to the punishment of sins. The previous generations, being so holy and perfect were punished for the slightest sin. But the minor sins do not make any impression on us who are immersed in so many sins. So the Lord overlooks them.

However slander caused a lot of trouble in the world. The snake has spoken evil against the Lord, consequently he brought death in the world.

Our Rabbis have compared the slanderer to the snake. When all animals attack and devour their prey they derive pleasure from that action as they satiate their hunger. The snake, however, harms or even kills his victim without deriving any benefit; he is like the slanderer in this respect. Joseph slandered his brothers, resulting in the exile of his family into Egypt. Datan and Aviram slandered Moses, which resulted in their sudden deaths. Miriam spoke against Zipora, and she was punished with leprosy. Our second Temple was destroyed because of the hatred between Kamtza and Bar-Kamtza.

During his cleansing the leper had to bring two birds as a sacrifice. The reason given is that he was, as it were, twittering like a bird, never stopped talking, and could not control his tongue which had broken through the two natural barriers, the lips and teeth. This proved that he was unable to control his wickedness.

Part of his cleansing was also cedar wood. It is a strong wood. In life we have witnessed how even strong persons have been destroyed and demolished through blackmail and lies – being undermined and broken by vicious and poisonous people.

Bar-Kochva made a fatal blunder by listening to slander. By nature the slanderer is an egoist who wants to build himself up by degrading others. He wants to be the cedar tree whilst others should be the hyssop.

Our Rabbis said, however: "Be soft like a reed and not hard like the cedar tree".

The blackmailer does his evil work secretly and quietly, like the scarlet worm; he therefore had to bring scarlet and hyssop.

The leper had to visit the high priest. The latter had to be a true leader, and had to cure the victim's spiritual malady and show him the correct way with patience and real love. He was not to discourage and estrange him and push him away as the prophet Elisha had done to Gachazei. After being cursed by Elisha Gachazei became leprous. Disenchanted with his teacher Elisha, he helped Joravam with the golden calves. Apparently he knew about magnetism, so he helped him to deceive the people by pulling them up into the air through magnetism. The people, on seeing the golden calves hanging in the air, started to believe in them and so he misled the people of Israel.

Our Rabbis said: "Push him away with the left hand but bring him to you with the right hand". In other words, the encouragement has to be more than the discouragement. Another saying must be remembered: "Be gentle with the youth, soft words subdue the anger".

These are the correct qualities of a leader.

ACHAREI-MOT

(16-1) "And the Lord spoke unto Moses after the death of the two sons of Aaron": One of the reasons given by the Rabbis for their punishment was that they had been intoxicated when they had entered the Holy Temple.

People may be intoxicated with alcohol, while others may become drunk with egoism, pomposity and pride. It was rather with that kind of self-deception that they became intoxicated; and as a result they did not give the required respect to their elders. For that reason they also remained bachelors, as all the girls who were proposed to them for marriage were discarded and rejected as not being suitable enough for their worth and importance. The question, however, is: Why such a severe punishment, it is not commensurate with their sin? The answer is provided in the verse: "They were near to the Lord".

If an ordinary person would have committed a sin like this, he would have been forgiven. But because they were important and in daily contact with the holiness of the Temple, it was expected of them to act precisely and impeccably. Because of that the anger of the Lord was directed upon them.

(16-2) "Speak unto Aaron thy brother". He had to warn Aaron that he may not assume that, because he was his brother he may do whatever he liked. He would do whatever he liked and then Moses would intervene with prayers which would be so effective that his sins would be forgiven as the Lord had forgiven them for the sin of the golden calf. So the Lord told him in simple terms: "Do not be misled although he is your brother"; but there is no prejudice and bribery in the presence of the Lord.

The tragedy of the death of his two sons really broke Aaron. It lingered in his mind till the last days of his life. After that Aaron removed himself from public life and hardly dared to intervene in any controversial communal disputes. Even in the unsuccessful uprising of Korech he stood aside. That was what Moses said (16-11): "And as to Aaron what is he that ye murmur against him, he is certainly innocent". Moses took all the blame upon himself. We read this portion on Yom Kippur in order to warn us about our behaviour, deeds and actions – our way of life has to be decent and correct.

K'DOSHIM

(19-1) "And the Lord spoke unto Moses saying: 'Speak unto all the congregation of the children of Israel. Ye shall be holy!'" Normally the Bible writes "to the Children of Israel", but here it is changed to "the congregation" – because to be holy one needs an environment for the individual is influenced by his environment. If the environment is indifferent to religion it automatically affects the individual. The singular is part of the plural, therefore Rashi states that the sidra of Kdoshim was addressed to the public. The public sets the tone and fashion for the environment.

One of the Rabbis has remarked that the opening verses of the Sidra state three times consecutively: "I am the Lord your G-d".

There are three categories of Jews, one who is very strict in his observance, that even the most minute details of the commandment are not overlooked. The second category is not so strict in the observance, however Shabbat and respect for their parents are observed. The third one is that even Shabbat is not observed but they have not converted. However, all of them are Jews and there is great hope for all of them. The Sidra enumerates the various elements which are, as it were, the ingredients of holiness. To support and help the poor, "you may not steal". There is an association between the above two injunctions. There are people who in business are cheating, stealing and deceiving many poor people on the assumption that charity will ultimately forgive and obliterate their sins. That is a stupid mistake. The prophets have already warned the people about that tragic self-deception.

The Torah also indicates that if the rich will not support the poor then the latter, in desperation, may become thieves, which is indirectly the fault of the rich.

"May not tell a lie". "A liar," said our Sages, "is worse than a thief". The latter steals money whereas a liar steals your confidence and peace of mind. A thief does his work secretly whereas the liar does his work openly and secretly.

We are responsible for one another, which is also part of our holiness, therefore we were instructed "thou shalt surely rebuke thy neighbour". The Torah twice repeats the word "rebuke". The Talmud (Bava Metzia 24) gives a reason for the repetition: "you have to rebuke your friend even a hundred times. If you were unsuccessful the first time, you may succeed the second time". As the Talmud says, the older learned people get the wiser they become. It may also be interpreted as advice to preachers. If you think that it is necessary to rebuke, divide your criticism into a hundred parts, but do not pour out the anger in one go. Rather do it gradually and methodically, in this way it may sink in more effectively and usefully.

Do not hate your brother, rather love him. Even if your friend does not conduct himself correctly yet do not despise him. In the same manner as you like yourself with all your faults – similarly you have to love your friends, for whatever he stands for.

A person who conforms to the above description is suitable to be a preacher. First cleanse yourself and then you will cleanse others.

EMOR

(21-1) "And the Lord said unto Moses speak unto the priests and say unto them". The Rabbis have remarked on the repetition of "speak and say", which they explained as follows: it was a command to the elders to look after the youngsters; it is the duty of the parents to educate their children and not to rely on others to do so, according to Deut. (6-7): "And thou shalt teach them diligently unto thy children". The teacher acts as a proxy for his parents, but the parents are not absolved from their duties to supervise even when teachers are known to perform their tasks capably and sincerely.

According to our Rabbis: if the teacher is like an angel then you may engage him. This may be interpreted as meaning that an angel performs one duty at a time; he concentrates and dedicates himself to one function only, therefore it is carried out punctually and impeccably. The same applies to a teacher. He has to be constantly mindful of the great responsibility entrusted to him. He may not act insincerely. The Ramban has stated that even a child before Bar mitzvah is not allowed to be given treif food nor allowed to desecrate Shabbat.

As that is all part of the education and upbringing of the child, he has to be guided and directed from childhood.

King Solomon says: bring up the child according to his way; meaning that there are neither uniformity nor strict rules in education. Every child has to be studied to find the suitable way to educate him. It is incumbent upon the teacher to probe the understanding and capabilities of the student as well as his environment and family background before the actual teaching may begin. It may also be interpreted that it is the duty of the great and famous leaders to teach and educate the youngsters – it is not below their dignity.

The Talmud (Bava-Batra 6) tells us that the great Tana Rabbi Yehoshua and Ben-Gamliel acted as teachers.

(Shabat 119) quotes Rav Hamnuna as saying that Jerusalem was destroyed because they abolished the teaching of children. Kings Yehoshafat and Hazkeyahu are said to have acted as teachers. Some commentators have remarked on the fact that normally the Lord directed his injunctions to Aaron whereas here Moses is commanded to speak to the children of Aaron, which may be explained in the following manner: the time of the injunction took place after the death of Aaron's sons, so if the Lord would have spoken to him directly he would possibly have felt a sense of guilt for their death which was perhaps due to his neglect of their upbringing. So in order not to put him to shame, the Lord addressed Moses about Aaron's children. The Lord subsequently singled him out very specially by commanding that the High Priest may not even attend the funeral of his parents. For the High Priest did not belong to his family; he was totally in the service of the people. All his worries and concerns had to be directed only and solely to the welfare of the nation. To emphasize that the Torah decreed that even in time of grief he was not allowed to permit his personal feelings to be dominant. He is not allowed to come in contact with a corpse and is even forbidden to attend to the needs of his own family.

Around the Tents of Torah

BHAR

(25-20) "When you come into the land which I give you then shall the land keep a Sabbath unto the Lord".

"Six years thou shall sow your field. But on the seventh there shall be a sabbath of solemn rest for the land. And if you shall say, what shall we eat the seventh year? Behold we may not sow, then I will command my blessing upon you in the sixth year, and it shall bring forth for the three years". At first glance the question "What shall we eat in the seventh year?" is difficult to understand, because in the seventh year they will still have food from the sixth year. Such a question could be valid for the eighth year; the fields will not have been worked on the seventh year.

The answer to such a query may be found in the nature and psychology of people. It is the rich and affluent person who possesses much who is more afraid and nervous about hunger and poverty than the poor person. We see it in the fact that there are many rich people who desecrate the Shabbat with the banal excuse that they have to make a living, which is in fact a travesty of the truth. They have so much that even if they would retire immediately they would still have sufficient funds even for their grandchildren. In Eastern Europe where poverty was so conspicuous our brethren observed Shabbat and were not afraid of starvation, because they had confidence and trust in the Almighty.

The verse, therefore, states that precisely in the seventh year when they will still have enough food the fear for the future will be expressed more than in the eighth year.

A story is told about the Gaon Rabbi Chaim of Volozhin, whom a rich person had asked for a blessing as he was about to embark upon a new business enterprise and was anxious about the prospects. The Gaon consented and blessed him. Later the person came to the Gaon with the following explanation: "Rabbi, now I see that there is a Lord in the world, for your blessing was realised". To which the Gaon replied:

"Here lies the difference between the rich and the poor; while the latter sees the Lord every day the rich sees Him once in a lifetime!"

The Torah promised us that there will be sufficient food and grain for three years. From that we may gauge that the Torah was given to us by the Lord and not by Moses. Because no King or Ruler would have risked to issue such a definite statement – to leave the fields barren for a year whilst the previous year's harvest will definitely provide for the following three years. Such a firm undertaking is beyond the powers and capabilities of a human being. How can one predict that a particular year will yield an abundance of grain, sufficient to provide food for the population? It may very likely be otherwise and a famine will follow which may cause an upheaval in the land ending in revolution and violent change.

This certainly shows that the law was truly given by the Lord, just as the whole of the Torah was given to us by the Lord.

During the sabbatical year, the poor man and the rich were equal. The rich farmer was forbidden to enclose or fence his field to prevent the poor from picking the fruit which grew without sowing. The poor did not feel humbled in the presence of the wealthy. During that year the people had an opportunity to devote their time to the service of the Lord; and meditation would lead to penitence. The Shmita – the sabbatical year – annuls debts. This law is observed even in the Diaspora unless a Pruzbul is written before which grants permission to collect debts. The sabbatical year fills every Jew with the realisation that there is a Lord who guides and directs the world. In the Talmud (Sanhedrin 39) the disciple said: "What is the reason for 'Shmita'? The Lord said to the Hebrews, sow six years and leave out the seventh so that you will know that the land belongs to me. That results in trust in the Lord".

B'CHUKOTAI

(21-3) "If you will walk in my statutes"; Rashi adds, "to walk in my statutes" signifies that you will exert yourself to study the Torah. This may explain what King David said in Psalm 119-59 – "I considered my ways and turned my feet unto thy testimonies, I made haste and delayed not to observe thy commandments".

The Yalkut adds to this as follows: David said – "I was considering and thinking where to go and visit, however my feet instinctively led me to the house of learning".

It had become natural to him that his feet would lead to a holy place in order to serve the Lord. However, to attain such a high degree of integrity one would have to study diligently for many years. This explains the expression: "if you walk in my statutes". How can a person walk in statutes? We may understand this from the example of David. His feet as it were were accustomed to worship the Lord; they automatically brought him into the holy temple. But to achieve such a high degree of faith great devotion is required. "You will walk in my statutes" will become a natural habit to a person but for that, adds Rashi, one will have to exercise great effort.

(26-14-15) "But if ye will not hearken unto Me and will not do all those commandments and if you will reject my statutes". One is required to consider the last expression carefully for it is very significant. The text could have read: "and if you will not walk in my statutes" instead of saying "You will reject" them. In religion and faith there is no middle way. There are believers and atheists and if one does not believe one starts to hate and despise religion.

Rabbi Akiva corroborated this when he said that while he was a shepherd he would have bitten like a donkey, the believer. The Gaon compared this situation to a person who was being dragged out from a pit by a rope. If the hold on the rope were released the person would not remain hanging in the air, he would certainly drop down. The same principle applies to faith; either one goes up or falls down to the lowest stage of belief, breaks the covenant and abhors it.

However, the Lord warned us about the punishment which would follow. The text says "you will be driven like a leaf"; now a leaf is hit from both sides. It is first attacked from outside by the wind and then by other leaves similarly driven about in the air.

This is what has happened to us. We have been persecuted from without by our enemies and from within by our own brethren and the knock which comes from within is the more painful and the more telling. There is a story in the Midrash that when the Lord created man the trees in the forest became nervous and frightened because the axe might destroy them, so an old tree comforted them and said: "Friends, the axe needs a handle and we will have to provide it. If unity will exist among us and no one will give the handle then the axe is powerless". That is the power of unity and brotherhood among our people which is imperative for our survival.

BAMIDBAR

"And the Lord spoke to Moses in the desert of Sinai": The Midrash tells that the Torah was given through water, fire and desert. Our sages pointed out that the Torah contains the special quality of water, whereby it flows down from the mountains and collects in the valleys. So is it with the Torah; it leaves the egoistical person who is eaten with pride and lands among the humble and simple people. We may also add that there are no barriers for water. It may become a mighty force which breaks down obstacles and finally finds a path far from its destination. So it is with the Torah. The Lord promised us that the Torah would not be forgotten among

Israel and indeed we witness it even in our generation. Our faith breaks through family and environmental barriers and obstacles even from homes where parents know nothing about Judaism. Out of spite of that complete ignorance the child becomes religious and forces even the parents to change their attitude towards Judaism. Presumably this is what the prophet Isaiah (Chap. 11-9) may have referred to when he said: "For the earth shall be full of the knowledge of the Lord, as the waters cover the sea". It is the eternity of our Torah which will prevail for ever.

There is also another interesting aspect concerning water. Mighty rivers and stormy seas are after all only numberless small drops of water. They are united beyond recognition – millions of them are gathered into one place, eventually to become great waters which may break through and flood everything in their way. The same principle applies to our religion. The future of our faith lies in complete unity. Every Jewish believer, if he is not affiliated as a member of a religious body, is powerless to stand up against the streams of agnostic ideology. But if we stand united in faith and courage then we may become a power which will resist all the attacks directed against our beliefs.

For that, order and organisation are necessary. The Torah tells us that while the Israelites were travelling in the desert they proceeded according to their appointed flags – each person to his job and work. They had to guard everything jealously, to watch and to supervise; that is to guard and watch constantly those of our religious enemies whose main aim and desire is our religious destruction.

By Fire: The Lord appeared to Moses in fire at the burning bush. The Torah was given to us on Mount Sinai in fire. The light of the Torah will eventually drive away the darkness of wickedness. Even one light can achieve a great deal, hence a religious person may never give up hope, because in the final analysis the truth will triumph over falsehood.

Fire may bring goodness and blessing; it brings light and warmth. But if one is not careful with fire it may cause destruction. It is the same with the Torah. If we fulfil the commandments with love and conviction then we shall reap happiness and contentment, but if we deviate from the right path and neglect the Torah it may bring about exile and destruction.

In the desert: The Torah is ownerless like the desert; there is no monopoly over it; it does not belong to any particular tribe or family. It is not confined to the righteous and to the prophets only.

Our Rabbis have said that a mamzer who is a scholar has preference over an ignoramus who may be a priest. The famous Tanaim Shmaia and Avtalian were descendants of non-Jews and yet were revered and greatly respected. "Be careful with the poor, for from them the words of our Torah will come forth". There may not be any prejudices or favouritism; the Torah belongs to all the people of Israel. Whoever desires may come forward and try to wear the crown of the Torah without any difference or distinction. Moses said: "You are all standing before the Lord, your wood choppers and water drawers". The Torah was given purposely in the desert for the following reason: Had the Torah been given in Jerusalem then the coming generation would have argued and said – "Yes! In Jerusalem which is a holy and pure place, there it is possible to observe and keep properly Judaism for the conditions are conducive to its observance. But we are living under difficult and discouraging conditions so we cannot remain strictly observant Jews". Hence the Torah was given in the desert to impress upon us that even in a spiritual desert we still can remain true religious Jews, wholeheartedly devoted to our holy and precious Torah. We have to show our will and determination that we are sincere in our belief. In this connection our Rabbis have said: "In the road which a person wants to go the Lord helps and leads him to real happiness and success".

Around the Tents of Torah

NASO

The Sidra of Naso is the longest one in the Bible, containing 176 verses. The longest chapter in Psalms (119) also contains 176 verses and the longest M'sichta in the Talmud Bava Batra is similarly composed of 176 pages.

Normally we read this Sidra on the festival of Shavuot for it may be considered symbolically. This is how we should accept our Torah. We should not curtail the prayers or diminish our studies. In Brachot (60) our Rabbis said: "On every day the Torah has to be looked upon as new, as on the day it was given to us". Take the sum of the sons of Gershon also – The Lord has commanded the enumeration and counting of the people of Israel. Also to allocate and to distribute the various duties and work which had to be accomplished and done by specially appointed and nominated personnel. The Sidra starts with the work which had to be done by the sons of Gershon – there is a special reason for that. They did simple, unskilled manual labour yet they were treated with reverence and honour. They were equal in the eyes of the Lord with those who did the holiest work like the attending to the holy Ark.

Verse 24 repeats this: "These are the work of the family of Gershon to work and carry the load".

The Torah has invariably honoured the labourer for he makes a living by the sweat of his brow.

The Lord placed Adam in the Garden of Eden and commanded him to work.

Gen. (2-15) "Through work and toil he would develop the garden". In Ethics our Rabbis urged all to love the work. Rabbi Meir in Kiddushin (84) said that a father has to teach his son a profession, to which Rabbi Yehuda added tailoring.

The Sidra contains various subjects which apparently do not seem to be correlated with one another. However, if we examine them deeply we can see that the common denominator and theme of the Sidra is organisation and order. Rabbi Eliezer says in the Talmud (Ktubot 60): "Idleness causes immorality". Rabim Shimon says it is insanity. When the people travelled according to their flags, Moses divided them according to their capabilities and aptitudes. The same is also necessary to insist on a useful order in our private activities. We have to educate and bring up our youth in a responsible way so that they are made aware of their responsibilities. They have to play their part in society and to share in all the burdens and problems of life. Failing that, they may become thieves and robbers which is one of the subjects dealt with in the Sidra.

The Sidra also deals with the Nazir, a person makes a vow to abstain from any kind of alcohol. Our Rabbis said in Talmud (Nazir) that if a person feels that he is being overpowered by wicked inclinations, he has to become a "nazir" in order to contain them which is again a part of our order in society. The order and self-discipline of the individual is very important in the structure of society. He has to be in order with himself. And so with his family life. When a woman is idle it may cause unfaithfulness or suspicion of it, which is another theme in the Sidra – "Sota".

The Sidra concludes with the blessing by the Priests – "The Lord will bless you and guard you". Rashi interprets in this manner: He will bless you with money and guard you from evil spirits. We occasionally find that when a person is blessed with riches and does not utilise the money for the benefit of society, he may eventually become an evil spirit to himself and to his environment. The wealth which was given to him by the Lord to help people has remained idle – moral and spiritual idleness is the result together with demoralisation. So the Priests' blessing in the name of the Lord is that He may guard us against the breaking of religious and spiritual order. Every person has to travel through life according to his appointed flag and specified order, given to us by the Lord.

Around the Tents of Torah

B'HAALUTCHA

(8-1) "Speak unto Aaron and say unto him, When thou lightest the lamps and the seven lamps shall give lighting front of the candlestick". The text uses a special word "B'haalotcha" which means literally "to uplift", signifying that the Lord has decreed Aaron to carry out the commandment of lighting the candles with alacrity and spiritual elevation. Through this warmth and enthusiasm he will be able to understand the hidden reasons involved in the lighting of the Menora.

In the same strain we may also understand the words of the Rashi. Aaron was upset when he was left out of the induction of the Mishkan. Everyone brought a sacrifice but Aaron did not participate, so naturally he was hurt and felt out of place so the Lord comforted him by saying: "Your offspring, the Maccabeans, will have the greater honour of lighting the candles and bringing sacrifices in the Second Temple.

Superficially it seems a small comfort to Aaron, for this compensation would only come after many generations.

However, looking at it from a broader historical point of view the reward was really stupendous. We see it very often when an induction of a synagogue takes place. The celebration is usually a great success, it is well attended, people donate enthusiastically, everyone is excited. Unfortunately the following day there may hardly be a Minyan. In some cases they have to hire people for the service. The question obviously occurs to one: where are those people who have packed the Shul yesterday? The answer is simple: some of the people came because of certain honours which were bestowed upon them or simply to witness a celebration half-heartedly, out of curiosity. Therefore their dedication evaporated so quickly.

Aaron's dedication, however, was different. He lit the candles with so much warmth and sincerity that his influence and greatness made an indelible impression upon his children and grandchildren and moved them to carry out the commandments of the Lord with self-sacrifice. His grandson, Pinchas, endangered his life when he killed Zimri. Moreover, his example proved to be unending, and has actually inspired many generations. It had an effect on the Maccabeans who fought with tenacity and courage against the Greeks and their followers among the Hebrews, and triumphed. Although their numbers were small, they relied upon the Lord, taking the greatness of Aaron as their example.

The Menora was hammered out of one piece of gold: the Lord had shown Moses a golden Menora made out of fire.

This is to signify that our religion has to be of one piece and entity: we are not allowed to reform or break it up. Just as when one breaks off a small piece of a precious Menora and causes it to lose its value, so with our religion. We may not dare to touch it or deviate from it because it may result in assimilation and chaos.

Reform is unfortunately progressing among those Jewish communities in these days when ignorance is the order of the day.

In the pre-war Poland, Lithuania, etc., reform could not make much progress because the Jewish people of those communities were versed in our Torah and knew a great deal of our religion. To them reform looked ridiculous and comical. Either one believed or disbelieved, but it cannot be commercialised and cut into pieces. Therefore the Lord had shown him a Menora made out of fire, implying that a precept of the Torah had to be carried out with conviction and deep concentration. Similarly when a teacher imparts his knowledge to his pupils, he has to do so with sincerity and integrity.

It is in this sense that we may interpret the saying of the Rabbis that Aaron did not change one iota of what he was told by the Lord to do, as the text corroborates and Aaron did accordingly; meaning that in spite of the difficulties which he encountered while carrying out his duties of lighting the candles, he still accomplished his holy work, never giving up hope of keeping the lights of the Tora burning. It was never extinguished, which is thanks to the Almighty. The ringing voice of the Torah is still heard in the Yeshivot and Synagogues – it is the voice of eternity.

SHLACH

(13-1) "And the Lord spoke unto Moses saying – Send to you men". Many commentators have already remarked about the phrase "to you" which seems to be unnecessary. The Yalkut, however, explains it in the following manner: The Israelites approached Moses and urged him to send men to spy out the land and gave him these reasons for their proposal. The Lord had promised the land to the children of Israel and they wished to enter and take possession of all its riches and goodness. (Deu. 6)

If the inhabitants might hear of their coming they would hide or take away all the treasures and consequently nothing would be left for them. This would mean that the promise of the Lord would not be fulfilled. For this purpose they wanted Moses to let them go into the land to prevent this from taking place.

It is to be noted that it was their intention to enrich themselves with silver and gold. The spiritual factors of the whole venture were of no concern to them. They wanted to find out whether there were trees therein or not. Nu. (13-20), on which Rashi comments that this means whether there were righteous people in the land.

The Lord had warned them that if their main aim in life was to acquire material gain only then the consequences might be tragic. Of course Moses was not interested in financial gain. He did not even take any part of the land in Israel. As we note from his words to Korah: "I have not taken one ass from them". This is why the Lord said "to you" in this verse, implying that the spies have to be "like you" – unselfish, concerned only about the community and the people. It was also the rebuke which Caleb gave them.

"We shall ascend" (13-30), signifying their desire to ascend spiritually, to overcome pettiness and narrow-mindedness.

If they conquered within themselves the temptation of greed and jealousy, then they would certainly reach their goal.

They would succeed in entering the land to build a strong nation, physically and spiritually.

Caleb continued, saying "they are bread for us". These words are difficult to understand, but they may be explained in this manner: When one studies the history of war, one fact becomes salient; when soldiers fight for the sole purpose of enriching themselves they will be victorious if no strong opposition is offered them. But once they meet strong and mighty adversaries who will fight bravely, then they desert their position and run away from the battlefield. However, when the soldiers are hungry and starving, they go into battle in order to obtain enough food to satisfy their hunger. Soldiers in such a position will fight with great determination; nothing in the world will stop them. In this context what Caleb said may be interpreted as follows: "To us, to own a land, to be independent, is like bread for the hungry. You have witnessed what happened to us in Egypt where they oppressed and killed us and our children were drowned or strangled. Certainly the Lord will help us".

But the people did not listen but argued and complained. Therefore the Lord punished them by condemning them to perish in the desert. The Lord did not forgive them. A people that does not appreciate and love freedom and independence does not deserve to possess a land and be free. Moses intervened on their behalf and asked for forgiveness but without success.

Some commentators ask why the sin of the golden calf, which was a great crime against the Lord, was forgiven them after the intervention of Moses but the sin of the spies was not forgiven in spite of the pleading of Moses.

There is a logical answer to this question. The sin of the golden calf was a confrontation with the Lord only, so even though the sin was great, the Lord forgave them. But the sin of the spies was a crime against the future of Israel as well and that the Lord could not forgive. The old generation had to die in the desert and the young generation would enter and build the land (14-31): "But your little ones that you said would be a prey, them will I bring in and they shall know the land which ye have rejected".

We have witnessed a similar phenomenon in our own times. The young generation whom we regarded as assimilated and lost to us because, unfortunately, many of them had not received sufficient religious education and upbringing, were the pioneers in the land of Israel who have sacrificed their lives on the altar of our nation. They were the vanguard who, with the help of the Lord, prepared a refuge for our unfortunate brethren fleeing from the fire of hell which nearly annihilated us. They have known the land!

KORAH

(16-1) "And he took Korah the son of Izhar ... " The verse does not state what he took and there are various interpretations of the verse. Onkelos translates "And he quarrelled"; Targum Yerushalmi translates "And he took advice". But actually all the translations contain one common denominator, namely the possibility of dissension and trouble. To disrupt the people, organisation and scheming were necessary. Because of jealousy Korah had long decided to carry out a revolution but was waiting for the right opportunity to come out into the open with his diabolic plan; so he "took advice" in order to lay his plans carefully. According to his calculations the time now appeared to be ripe. It was after the tragic incident of the spies, as a consequence of which the Israelites were punished to wander for forty years in the desert. Naturally the people were disappointed and enraged. The discontent grew the more after the failure of the tribe of Ephraim to go up on their own to Israel. The disaster ended in all of them being massacred. This is known as the "Maapilim Episode".

Korah, therefore, decided to exploit the favourable circumstances and the explosive feelings of the people and began to realise his long-cherished ambition. In the beginning he was successful in gathering around him frustrated, angry and dissatisfied elements, who were hungry for honour and publicity; these were jealous and unpopular people. Korah took them in by inciting them against Moses. That is known as the rage of Korah and his congregation.

And he said (16-13): "Is it a small thing that thou hast brought us up out of a land flowing with milk and honey to kill us in the wilderness". It is difficult to understand this complaint. How could they describe Egypt as a land of milk and honey? Had they not forgotten how they were oppressed and their children cast in the river? But such is the power of controversy; it blinds and misleads even the cleverest of people. Our Rabbis pointedly asked how it could have happened to Korah who was a clever person. The answer they gave was that his eye misled him. It is the eye of ambition which is responsible for his downfall. As the Rabbis say in Ethics (4-28): "Stupidity, jealousy and ambition take a man from the world".

Korah chased after honours, he was envious and coveted riches and wealth. This enticed him from the correct and true road of life.

Moses was very much grieved and tried with all his skill to bring about peace. However, they kept to their crooked and wicked path.

Around the Tents of Torah

The Lord punished them in a strange manner; He caused the earth to swallow them up. It was measure for measure. They wanted to climb to the highest place in society, to rule and to oppress the people, so the Lord degraded and cast them down. Our Rabbis in Sanhedrin state that Korah and his congregants are still shouting from their graves.

We may explain this allegorically: Arguments and quarrels which bring destruction and calamity in their wake are not obliterated and forgotten quickly. Even after the punishment has been meted out the effects are still apparent. The accusations and the lies still fly around as it were; the air is still, filled with hypocrisy and falsehood. So in this case Korah still had a following.

After Korah was swallowed up the Lord commanded Moses to place twelve rods in the Holy Tent.

(17-23) "And it came to pass on the morrow that Moses went into the tent of the testimony and behold the rod of Aaron for the house of Levi was budded and put forth buds and bloomed blossoms and bore ripe almonds". This miracle contradicted the whole supposition made by Korah who said that our Torah was old and not relevant to the times. The miracle proved that our Torah is constantly fresh and new, always in a state of flowering and blossoming.

Although Korah died his children are still alive to this very day. We still find some of our people who "grumble and complain against Moses". That is borne out in a lighter vein.

In the first verse "And Korah took" Rashi comments that that portion is well interpreted and explains: When a preacher comes into a town to deliver a sermon to an audience whom he does not know, he may sometimes tread on dangerous ground.

He may take a theme about the observance of Shabbat or Kashrut and rebuke them for their negligence. After the sermon a person may come up to him saying: "Excuse me, preacher, you made a mistake. We all observe the Shabbat and Kashrut". But if he will take his theme, disunity and dissension in the community, none of the audience will make him aware of the irrelevance of his sermon because the children of Korah are still very much alive, which is a sad feature. May the Lord help us!

HUKAT

(19-1) "And the Lord spoke unto Moses and unto Aaron saying: 'This is the statute of the law which the Lord hath commanded saying Speak unto the children of Israel that they bring thee a red heifer'." This sacrifice cleansed the unclean, those who had come into contact with a dead body. It was a paradoxical sacrifice because the Cohen who administered the cleansing became unclean himself!

It was one of those laws which we had to fulfil as it were blindly without asking questions. As Rashi comments – "it is a decree from the Lord, you have no right to query".

Our Rabbis, however, have offered some explanations: "Let come the mother and make amends for her son", that is, let the heifer come and make amends for the calf! The sin of the golden calf was great and incomprehensible. After receiving the Torah and pledging "we shall do and listen", the People of Israel went and made a golden calf! Commentators have ventured the view that it was actually these Egyptians who had become half-hearted Jews, who were responsible for the construction of the calf. Nevertheless the fact is that very many of the Israelites actively participated in this backsliding. How else was it possible for a sin like this to be committed? Moreover the Lord did not forgive them completely for He said (Exo. 32-34): "Nevertheless in the day when I visit,

I will visit their sin upon them". From this it is obvious that the anger of the Lord was still kindled against them because it had been a treacherous rebellion against the Lord and Moses. They had exchanged the Lord for an idol. But when we delve more deeply into the spiritual circumstances in which the Israelites found themselves we may find an excuse for their sinful behaviour.

(1) After being in Egypt for 210 years, they were subconsciously affected by the idol-worshipping majority of the population. To some extent the parents were also responsible by not bringing up their children correctly. The fathers may be excused for the shortcomings in the education of their children because they were slaves who worked hard making bricks, but not the mothers. They may be blamed for neglecting the spiritual needs of their children because being home they could have guided them in the correct way. That is indicated by our Rabbis who said: "Let the mother make amends for the child". Education is also in the same paradoxical condition: it may cleanse the unclean but it may also make unclean the clean. If there is a real religious education and the pupils are taught Judaism and our pure faith with sincerity, then the children will grow up to be proud and observant Jews. But if the teachers themselves are atheists or hypocrites who do not believe in their own teachings, then even the clean ones become unclean.

The same principle applies to money. With money we can acquire worthy objectives – the spreading and teaching of Torah, helping Israel, and the giving of charity; but unfortunately money also causes trouble, revolution and murder.

(20-1) "And Miriam died there and was buried there". There is an association between the death of Miriam and the red heifer. As mentioned, the sacrifice of the red heifer had no obvious reason; similarly we are puzzled about the death of righteous people. When a righteous person dies suddenly we start to wonder why did he die? But the law in life is that even righteous people die.

After the death of Miriam there was no water, the people started to complain. Moses lost his patience and exclaimed: "Listen you rebels!" and hit the rock. As a result Moses was punished: he would not enter the land because a leader must have patience and understanding. He should have acted like a father towards his children. Even when he is disappointed with them, the father's love is stronger and deeper than the pain and grief caused by his children. Yehoshua on the other hand showed patience and love in face of the provocation perpetrated by Achan who committed a great sin by taking some articles of Jericho, causing the Israelites suffering.

However, Yehoshua addressed him as "My son Achan". From that moment the Lord appointed him as a leader. Moses begged to be forgiven but to no avail. The Lord knew that the Israelites were stubborn but still they were his children even if they were spoilt and unruly. As the prophet says, "return you unruly children".

The Lord was positive that the people would return to him in time.

BALAK

(22-2) "And Balak the son of Zippor saw all that Israel had done to the Amorites". Our Rabbis have remarked that Balak was an ordinary person but was ambitious and ready to grab power. Eventually when the Israelites had conquered the Amorites he started like all inciters and demagogues to incite his people against the Israelites by spreading lies and falsehoods. He misled them by not revealing the truth that the Israelites actually wanted peace.

(20-21) "Let me pass through thy land. We will not turn aside into field or into vineyard". Rashi comments: "The Israelites were not supposed to suggest peace, yet they suggested peace". Sichon showed his audacity in that he did not even find it necessary to reply but immediately mobilised his army.

Balak however launched a campaign of vilification and lies that the Israelites were wild, cruel and uncivilised; who attacked and assaulted innocent people without any reason or provocation, grabbed and robbed other people's land and property.

The simple people believed him. History has repeated itself many times when it comes to hatred of the Jews. Somehow a people are found who will believe all the nonsensical accusations and foolish lies, even if contradicted by reality.

"Balak came to lick the blood of the Israelites" (Bal-Haturim). The last letters of "Ba-lak" and "lick" have the same sound.

"He rose and preached" (22-4). "Now will this multitude lick up all that is round about us as the ox licketh up the grass of the field".

Subsequently Balak became King over the Moav, whom he enchanted with his fine words which won him popularity.

Balak was now a captive because of his own blunders which he had perpetrated. He could not extricate himself from his own blunders so he had perforce to continue his anti-Israel policy. He, therefore, despatched messengers to Beelam who was a well-known Jew-baiter. He had once been a minister in Pharaoh's cabinet and was the one who had advised him to cast the Jewish children into the river. Our Rabbis say that the name Beelam may be interpreted as "Blo-am", without a nation, meaning that he was an international person. One can find a Jew-baiter among every nation and in each country whose hatred is poisonous like the venom of a snake.

Beelam consented to go (22-21). "And Beelam rose up in the morning and saddled his ass and went with the princes of Moab". Rashi comments: Abraham also rose up in the morning when the Lord told him to bring Isaac as a sacrifice (Gen. 22-3). "And Abraham rose early in the morning and saddled his ass". This shows that Beelam who was also a prophet, knew that the Lord would not forsake his people so he had to refuse to go, because the Lord would not allow anyone to harm His people. This is obvious from the fact that at the last moment when Abraham was prepared to slaughter his son, a voice came out and said: "Do not harm your son". Had the Lord desired the extinction of Israel He would have allowed Abraham to slaughter Isaac, so automatically there would have not been a Jewish nation. However, the fact that the Lord intervened and stopped Abraham from proceeding with his action of slaughtering his son, proves beyond doubt how great is the love of the Lord for Israel. Beelam, who was undoubtedly a wise person, at that moment lost his elementary logic and went with the emissaries of Balak.

The ass crushed Beelam's foot against the wall. By that Beelam was warned – "you are hurrying to do bad, but the Lord will prevent you from carrying out your wicked and cruel intentions and schemes". Then he began to hit the ass, hence the Lord opened the mouth of the ass and he said unto Beelam: "What have I done unto thee that thou hast smitten me these three times?" Beelam was again warned by this miracle. "You are boasting about your capabilities, that you are a fluent speaker who will succeed in cursing the Israelites. Beware! the Lord will silence you, there is nothing impossible for the Lord to achieve; the Lord can make the ass to speak and to silence you!"

And so it was, the Lord prevented him from carrying out his evil intentions. Instead of cursing he blessed them. At the end when he came to claim his reward he was killed in the war of Midian against Israel.

Our Rabbis commented on the verse (Deu. 34-10): "And there hath not arisen a prophet since in Israel, like unto Moses" by saying that among the non-Jews there was such a prophet, and it was Beelam!

This is difficult to understand. How can one compare these two prophets? Moses was the source of holiness, sanctity and kindness; Beelam was the root of all evil, a despicable person. The great Gaon Rabbi Chaim of Valozin provided a clever answer. There are two kings among the birds, the eagle and the owl, but with a difference. While the eagle is the King of the day, the owl is the King of the night and darkness. Moses was the King of light and goodness and kindness but Beelam was the King of darkness and defilement.

Balak had the honour of having a Sidra named after him. Why did he deserve it? The reason is that there are two kinds of Jew-baiters in the world: one of them superficially speaks about fair play towards us but secretly acts like a snake in the grass; the other at least does not pretend but is an open enemy. The first one is more dangerous and frightful to us than the other because we know how we stand with him. Balak showed his opposition and hatred openly, he was not a hypocrite. That in itself is of some advantage to us, therefore a Sidra was named after him.

PINCHAS

"Pinchas, the son of Eliezer the son of Aaron the High Priest". The Torah has again repeated the ancestry of Pinchas.

Rashi comments: Pinchas endangered his life by killing Zimri who had degraded the name and prestige of Israel by committing an immoral deed with a heathen woman openly. By his deed he saved the honour and dignity of the Israelites. However, the tribes started to abuse him so the Torah stated his ancestry again to stress his greatness, his descent from royalty.

This has unfortunately become a normal occurrence in our history. When a really great man appears on our national horizon with a truthful and helpful message to our people which would certainly be beneficial for our future, mediocre people will start to oppose him. A campaign of blackmail, virulent lies and a blasphemous propaganda will be launched to belittle and besmirch him, so as to undermine his influence.

But the Lord promised that He would grant him His covenant of peace, so his adversaries did not succeed in their wicked enterprise. The Lord also promised that nothing would happen to him if he would continue to criticise the people.

Normally some people are afraid to voice their critical opinions, for that might cause friction and animosity. The Lord, however, promised him Peace. If one does this for truth only, then even one's enemies will eventually recognise his true worth.

In Hebrew the word Shalom is spelled Shin Lamed Vav Mem but in the text the Vav is half of its normal size.

To indicate that extremeness is necessary and important for the survival of our nation, but that we have to be careful and cautious not to overstep the mark because sometimes the consequences may be tragic as it may cut and destroy the place, we have to think coolly and logically before indulging in an extreme course.

That is the reason for Moses' silence and inactivity. Zimri had previously insulted him personally, and if Moses would have killed him people might have said that it was done for personal reasons and not for the honour of the Lord.

"Phinehas, the son of Eleazar, the son of Aaron the priest, hath turned my wrath away from the children of Israel in that he was very jealous for My sake among them, so that I consumed not the children of Israel in My jealousy".

We had and have many Jewish revolutionaries and fighters for freedom and justice but they have used their energies and capabilities to free and liberate other nations. Their own race and people they ignored completely. They have brought sacrifices on the altar of nations, who later rejected them, but have intentionally forgotten their own cause and future. Phinehas, however, acted for our people and faith. According to our Rabbis he is Eliyahu, who will announce the coming of Messiah, the final redemption.

After the tragedy of Zimri when 24 000 people died by the plague the Lord ordered the people to be counted again; the letter "Hei" was added to the beginning of the name of each leader and a letter "yud" at the end; these are part of the name of the Lord! This signifies that if a person is pure in his youth and has done penance at his old age, the sins of the middle years are forgiven and he is finally accepted by the Lord. So, in spite of the sad fact that they had sinned with Zimri since they expressed their regret, the Lord forgave and reinstated them like righteous people.

Our Rabbis say that "in the place where people who have done penance are standing, righteous people cannot stand!" The reason is that a righteous person who has never tasted and experienced sin will not find it difficult to resist and abstain from doing evil and wicked deeds. But a past-sinner who knows the pleasures of life and yet stands by his convictions and belief – that is really great and noble and for this he deserves praise and a singular honour.

The Lord knew the nature and character of his people who were sometimes quarrelsome and envious, therefore he instructed Moses to divide the land according to lots, before they would enter it, in order to avoid recriminations and mutual accusations about the division of the land.

The Lord now told Moses that he would not enter the land. It was done with the special intention of avoiding unpleasantness for Moses. Some might have said that he was biased and prejudiced, but such accusations were not valid as Moses was not an interested party, who would benefit from that division.

Even the leadership he handed over to a stranger, not even to one of his tribe. Yehoshua belonged to the tribe of Ephraim, while

Moses was from the tribe of Levi. The Sidra concludes with the sacrifices, to emphasise that a leader must be prepared to bring sacrifices for the people.

Moses had toiled and devoted his life in order to educate and develop the people, but was not given the privilege of entering the land; that in itself was a great sacrifice on the altar of the people and land.

MATOT

The contents of the Sidra centre on one theme, namely that of fulfilling and carrying out of a promise which had been made either to the Lord or to the People, because the holiness, decency and future of a nation rests mainly upon the sanctity of promises and the holiness of a person's word of honour. Otherwise mutual confidence and trust are lost; suspicion, falsehood and treachery take their place.

The Sidra begins: "He shall not break his word, he shall do according to all that proceedeth out of his mouth". The Lord granted to human beings the talent of speech, by virtue of which he stands higher than animals. (Gen. 1-7) states: "And man became a living soul", concerning which Onkelos comments – "and man became a speaking spirit", saying it is the soul which enables him to speak, it is the spark from the Lord. It has therefore to be preserved in its purity and not to be defiled by lies, slander or blasphemy. "Do not make your word unholy" states the Torah.

Even if the promise was made to oneself, it still has to be carried out. Firstly, Moses addressed himself to the leaders, saying that it was incumbent upon them to keep their word; they had to show an example to the people, to carry out their promises made, and then only would they have the right to criticise others for their shortcomings and faults.

Moses had also personally kept a promise – to make war against Midian. Although he was aware that he would die on the termination of the battle as he had been forbidden to enter the land of Israel, yet he neither tarried nor postponed his last act, but went immediately into battle against the Midianim. So he proved that a promise had to be kept, even when detrimental to oneself.

Shabat (56) mentions Rabbi Yehuda as saying in the name of Rav that when King David said to M'fiboshet who was the son of Yehonatan, the son of King Saul – "you and Tsiva will divide the fields that is the inheritance", a voice came from heaven saying Rehavam and Yaravam will divide the kingdom and concludes that had David not accepted the lies of Tsiva, his kingdom would never have been divided and we would never have been exiled.

The explanation is as follows: David made a promise to Jonathan of mutual faithfulness (Samuel 20-42) – "we have sworn both of us in the name of the Lord saying the Lord shall be between me and thee and between my seed and thy seed forever", namely that he would watch over and care lovingly for the children of Jonathan to provide them all their requirements to enable them to live in honour and dignity. But on his return home from his exile, after having fled from his son Avshalom, Tsiva approached him with a false smile and succeeded in gaining the confidence of the King, telling him cunning lies about M'fiboshet. David accepted them hurriedly without investigating the correctness or otherwise of his accusations. In doing so David broke his promise and word and was the eventual cause of the division of his kingdom. On ascending to the throne Rehavam, the son of Shlomo, gathered around him young and inexperienced people who did not care about keeping promises. Breaking a vow was to them hardly material; and so the people lost their faith in them.

Subsequently when Joravam came and used his smooth and lying tongue, he succeeded in swaying the people and drew them after him. He gained the confidence of the ten tribes, the government of Rehavam was split, they lapsed into idol worship and were finally exiled – all the result of a broken promise.

The two and a half tribes had also made a promise that prior to their settlement in Transjordan, they would help their brethren to conquer Israel. After a misunderstanding they finally carried out their promise. Moses had spoken hard words to them (Num. 32-6): "Shall your brethren go to the war and shall ye sit here?" If there will not be peace in Israel, if there will not be security and tranquillity in the land, then our position in the Diaspora will also be in danger.

This has already been corroborated by history. The fate of Jewry in exile is linked with that of Israel. Their insecurity affects our own; their peace and security means the same to us.

MAASEY

(32-1) "These are the stages of the children of Israel by which they went forth out of the land of Egypt, by their hosts under the hand of Moses and Aaron".

In the course of the 40 years during which the People wandered they had 42 stations each of which had a reason and a purpose. They did not wander aimlessly like sheep without a shepherd, without supervision; but were guided by the two illustrious leaders, Moses and Aaron who watched over them with a loving eye.

Everything had been ordained by the Lord. (2) And Moses wrote their going forth to their travellings and later the order in the verse is reversed "and these are their travellings to their going forth". There is an explanation for this.

Normally when people travel they have a definite aim, that is "the going forth to their travellings", meaning that they are leaving their town, to proceed to a certain destination. However, there are times when people are obliged out of danger to flee from their native town but their destination is not known to them – their only aim is to leave the place which spells danger for them. In this case the text states, "their travellings to go forth" – their only interest is to get away from the danger zone. That is the reason for the changed word order in the verse.

The Torah enumerates the various names of the stations where the Israelites rested. The reason is given by the "More Nevuchim" in order to verify and corroborate the authenticity of the Bible, as those names have indeed been confirmed to be true by the archaeologists. In Elim they rested because there was water – they went in a hurry for lack of water, so we can see that the Torah even mentions the reason for their resting and departures.

An obvious question which follows from this is why did not the Bible record the reasons for their resting at Mount Sinai, which was to receive the Torah? The answer is that after the Torah had been given to us it was no longer confined to any particular place or time, but every place is its place, and the same is with time. We have to study the Torah every minute of the day. Accordingly we may explain the reason why nothing is mentioned about why we have to celebrate Shavuot.

The receiving of the Torah is completely omitted from the text. The answer is: The observance of all the other festivals are confined to a special date. We have to eat matzo during Pesach only, we have to sit in the Sukka during that festival only, but the study of the Torah is neither confined to nor allocated to a specific and special time or date: "you will meditate in the Torah, day and night".

After Moses had enumerated all their stages of travelling and reiterated all the difficulties and problems which they had encountered all those days, he told them when they entered Canaan it would be incumbent upon them to show their love and devotion by making sacrifices for their land.

(Num. 33-52) "Then you shall drive out all the inhabitants of the land from before you and destroy all their figured stones and destroy all their molten images and demolish all their high places". The Hebrew culture and faith had to be more convincing and stronger than the culture of the heathens as otherwise their victory would be in vain and of a temporary nature only. "They will remain as thorns in your eyes and as pricks in your sides and they shall harass you in the land wherein you dwell".

The women were not allocated any power in the land. They were excluded from inheritance, but if there were no sons then the daughters had the right to inherit. Consequently the families of the sons of Joseph came with a complaint to Moses about the daughters of Zelophehad who had no brothers. If they inherited and then married someone belonging to another tribe they would take long their inheritance with them. Consequently the land of the other tribe would increase and their own portion would decrease. Moses said the sons of Joseph spoke rightly, so he decreed that in the case of the daughters of Zelophehad they would have to marry within the tribe of Joseph.

The Even-Ezra comments that the leaders of the tribe of Joseph had spoken not only on their behalf but actually intervened for the benefit of all the other tribes. This pleased Moses immensely as it was a real and practical demonstration of unity among the people. Moses also prepared cities of refuge before his death. If someone killed a person unintentionally he would be able to seek refuge in these cities from the avenger of the blood. The killing may have been committed when a person was not fully responsible for his actions, and the murderer himself more often than not is equally sorry for his deeds. Moses worried about the ethical and spiritual quality of the people – he wanted to avoid the spilling of innocent blood.

DVARIM

(Deu. 1-1) "These are the words which Moses spoke unto all Israel beyond the Jordan". The Sifri asks: did Moses speak these words only? Did not he write the whole Torah? It is stated (Deu. 31-24) – "and it came to pass when Moses had made an end of writing the words of this law in a book until they were finished". The Sifri answers: "these are words of reproof and rebuke!"

Moses, throughout his lifetime, was careful not to rebuke his people but invariably spoke to them words of encouragement. He was aware that people by nature resent criticism and rebuke. Rabbi Tarfon (Eiruvin 16) says similarly: "the fact is that you will hardly find a person in this generation willing to accept and listen to rebuke, people normally run away from them". However, before his death even his opponents agreed to listen to him; they paid attention to his ideas and showed him respect and honour. Nevertheless he did not use harsh words, but confined himself to hints and short remarks.

The Talmud (Bava Metzia 31) has this explanation to offer: Lev (19-17) reads "rebuke, rebuke your friend!" Why this repetition? This is to emphasize that you may have to rebuke him even a hundred times. This is interpreted as meaning that even if there is a need for rebuke, do not pour it out at one time, but divide it into small portions, otherwise you will enrage him.

"Reprove not a scorner lest he hate thee, reprove a wise man and he will love them" (Pro 9-8); (1-7) "After he had smitten Sihan the king of the Amorites". To criticise is easy, so prior to criticism he has to demonstrate practical accomplishments and results. He first defeated Sihan, bringing them to the very threshold of the Land of Israel, and only then did he take the liberty of rebuking them gently as a father admonishes his children. "In the Arava he hinted at the sin which they had committed around Moab, with the idol Poar; again he referred to the sin which they had sinned when they complained" (Ex. 14-11) – "because there were no graves in Egypt, hast thou taken us away to die in the wilderness?"

The question here is obvious: The sin of Pear was after the sin of Suph and yet it is mentioned here first. Moses mentioned it intentionally. He wanted to begin with the greatest crime – the most heinous one – idol-worship about which our law enjoins us – "rather be killed than transgress". In practice, however, a person does not immediately commit a grave sin. There is actually a gradual process; at first one commits a minor offence and if one does not regret it, then he embarks on the road of sin with no return. He starts off with a sin which is as thin as a spider web but it becomes gradually thicker, until it is like the ropes of a wagon.

They began with silly complaints at Suph but in due course ended up with idol-worshipping. And Di-Zahab, meaning gold, a reference to the golden calf. It is mentioned last but actually took place at the beginning of their wanderings. Moses wanted to defend his people, saying that it was not entirely their fault, as the blame could be attributed to the money which the Lord had showered upon them abundantly; they had become an affluent society.

(1-12) "How can I myself alone bear your troubles and your burden and your strife?" The Yalkut remarks that Moses said: "How can I myself alone bear your cumbrance?" Isaiah exclaimed (1-21): "How is the faithful city become a harlot?" Jeremiah said ((Lamentation 1-1): "How doth the city sit solitary, that was full of people?"

Actually there is a connection running through the above sayings – one sin causes another sin and one mistake causes another one. If a person does not believe then he starts to seek other beliefs as the harlot is constantly on the look out for more men. Rashi comments that by "burden" Moses referred to the atheists. What is really the connection between burden and atheists? If a person is a believer then the fulfilment of a mitzva is a pleasurable and easy task. He does not complain that the prayer is too long and uninteresting but to the atheists everything is a burden, the commandments are too many, they have to be curtailed and reformed.

In our morning prayers, "Blessed are thou our Lord who commanded us to occupy ourselves with the words of the Law", we notice the word "occupy" which serves to emphasize that our attitude towards the study of Torah should be as our interest towards our occupation.

When a person has to attend to his business or financial matters he does so without complaining and grumbling. He does not bring up excuses about the weather, about his wife stopping him or any other health reasons. All these pretexts are generally non-existent when it comes to money matters. The same approach and attitude has to be employed when it concerns Torah matters.

(1-10) "Behold, ye, are this day as the stars of heaven for multitude". Just as each star follows its own path and does not encroach on or collide with other stars, so the people of Israel have to act and behave to avoid friction and clashes and to foster love and brotherhood among us.

VAETCHANAN

"And I besought the L-rd at that time saying". The Sifre comments: "After I had conquered the land of Sichon and Og, I thought that perhaps the decree prohibiting me from entering the land of Israel was abolished and annulled". After he had endangered his life in the battles Moses was now under the impression that his sins would perhaps be forgiven and permission granted to him to enter the land which he loved and cared for so much. In particular he longed and yearned to see Jerusalem – "The goodly hill country". Rashi interprets it as Jerusalem because the city stands spiritually upon a high standard of holiness and sanctity. It is from there that the word of the L-rd will come forth bringing justice to the world. "And the L-rd was wrath with me because of you".

The Sifre adds – "Rabbi Yehoshua says: 'As a woman who cannot bend because of her baby … '" (the text is Vayetaber; Ubor also means a baby). What is the connection with the text? It may be explained as follows: Our Rabbis say that had Moses entered the Holy Land then the Israelites would never have been exiled; his influence and greatness would have prevented this. Unfortunately, their spiritual standard was so low that they did not deserve to have such an illustrious and glorious leader as Moses. "Every leader according to the generation" is the saying. Moses, therefore, was punished because of his people. This is what the Sifre refers to as "baby". Moses was allegorically their spiritual father and mother. Parents are invariably ready to bring sacrifices for their children. As it were, the L-rd felt uncomfortable to punish Moses because of the Israelites. Thus the L-rd said to him: "Do not continue to speak to me about that". It was an unpleasant decision and ruling to make. Nonetheless, by his imploring to see the land, Moses added more glory to his greatness. He ascended to greater heights. Therefore the L-rd told him: "Ascend on the top of the Pisgah (mountain) and raise your eyes westwards and eastwards". First to the west which symbolises the periods of sunset, destruction and darkness of our long-suffering history, which will be followed, however, by days of sunrise, glory and praise. That will perhaps be achieved through the true and sincere leaders who may rise to great heights after his death. He was, therefore, commanded to strengthen and encourage Jehoshua who would lead them to final victory.

However, now they were sitting in the valley facing the idol Beth Peor; they were in a state of spiritual stagnation and frustration; their worship of Peor was a great disappointment and a betrayal of our faith. But Moses comforted them.

(4-4) "But ye that did cleave unto the L-rd are alive every one of you this day", implying that if you would make a real and sincere effort to believe in the L-rd, then they would be helped by Him. As our Rabbis say: "If a person desires to cleanse himself he is helped from above".

Historically speaking we have never distinguished ourselves militarily and physically except during the short period of King David's reign. Otherwise we never had mighty armies or strong navies. Our main claim to greatness was mainly our faith and Torah. Thus he said (4-6): "Observe therefore, and do them, for this is your wisdom and your understanding in the sight of the peoples". He also warned them (4-9): "Only take heed of thyself and keep thy soul diligently lest thou forget the things which thine eyes saw".

The late Gaon Rabbi Israel of Salant said that we normally look well after our health, and worry about the soul of others. Indeed it should be otherwise: we should worry about our own soul, to keep it clean and pure, and then look after the body and health of others. (11-15): "Take therefore good heed of your souls". When a person is sick then all the sweet food which he may eat will taste bitter to him. The fault obviously is due to his sick stomach. However, sometimes the sick person will blame the cook or those who are responsible for preparing the food. Similarly when we encounter spiritual sickness, some invariably try to find fault with our Torah, criticising and denigrating it. But unfortunately, the real fault lies with them for they have desecrated their soul and numbed their Jewish heart. Thus they have lost their feeling and taste of Judaism.

King David advises: "First taste and you will see". You will understand that the Torah is sweeter than the proverbial honey. "And you will seek from there your L-rd and you will find Him". Then you will truly understand the reasons of our faith and consequently you will acquire the correct taste. When you will seek it with all your heart and soul. The Torah is not an interesting story book. We have to exert ourselves to seek to understand the reasons and the holy words of the L-rd. In comparison to our Sages, we are like spiritual midgets. As our Rabbis have said that if they were like angels then we are at least human beings. However, if they were like men, then we are like asses. What we have to accept is that the L-rd is One.

It is beyond our comprehension to understand Him. We have to accept our pure faith as it was handed over to us by our forefathers and holy prophets.

EIKEV

(8-1) "All the commandments which I command thee this day shall ye observe to do, that ye may live and multiply and go in and possess the land which the Lord swore unto your fathers".

The commentators remark that the verse starts in the singular and ends in the plural, which is unusual. The answer may be that while studying the history of our people one salient point emerges, namely, that the start of our belief was made by an individual, namely Abraham. He was a lonely person who travelled from one place to another spreading the belief of monotheism. He was one person against a whole world, but eventually his teachings were acknowledged and recognised by humanity. We are also a minority who helped to teach the world the Bible. Today the results are encouraging, most of the people believe in the existence of the Lord. Therefore the verse starts in the singular, "I command you" which will be beneficial for the individual; the plural is for the people of the world.

"And he afflicted thee and suffered them to hunger and fed thee with manna". The comments of the Midrash Pliah is that from this one may learn that women have to light candles on the eve of Shabbat. What is the association? Another Rabbinic comment on the reason why they kept on complaining about the manna is that a blind person is not easily satiated for he does not see the food, and as the Israelites did not see the manna as proper food they kept on grumbling.

Why women have to light candles on the eve of Shabbat and other festivals has already been explained thus: The women have to expiate the sin which was committed by Eve. She enticed Adam to eat from the tree of knowledge; death came into the world and extinguished the light of life and it is the duty of women to relight it.

Actually Adam had a big choice of fruit to eat from, and he could have satiated his hunger and craving by eating others than the one he ate. So why did he transgress the commandment of the Lord? The answer is – he was spiritually and logically blinded; he did not understand that we have to curb our temptations and inclinations. At that moment his wisdom and common sense were blinded. He succumbed to the enticement of Eve and thereby brought sadness and sorrow upon him and the world; he failed to foresee the consequences. It was the same with the manna; if the Israelites would not have sinned then the manna would still have descended even after they had entered the land of Israel. But they lost their elementary judgement and became gluttons, and not being able to control their lust, they ate and were not satisfied; they were never satisfied with their possessions. As our Rabbis have said – if one has a hundred pieces he wants two hundred. Spiritual blindness was the root cause of the trouble. The reason for the stoppage of the manna and the lighting of the candles are then identical, namely their reason was dimmed and mind blinded. They had to realise that a man does not live by bread alone but by everything that proceeds out of the mouth of the Lord does man live. The cause of all these faults may be ascribed to their not having had a true religious upbringing. Hence the Torah's injunction to us "and you will teach your children".

The Yalkut asks: Why do your children die young? The answer is provided by the two sages, Rabbi Cheeya and Rabbi Yosi. The former says: "Because the neglect of the Mitzva of Mzuza", while the latter credits it to the abandonment of the study of Torah.

This may be explained allegorically as follows: we find that some of our youth are dying spiritually; they neglect our Torah and mock at our sanctity. What is the cause of this? One sage holds it is because of the neglect of Mzuza, which is the symbol of Jewishness proclaiming to the people that they should conduct themselves according to our faith and religion. The Mzuza contains the "Shma" – "Hear O Israel" – the belief in the love of the Lord. However, if that is missing or neglected, the result is the spiritual death of our children. The Rabbi maintains that the observance of Mitzvot is not sufficient; we must know the reasons for fulfilling them. An ignorant person cannot be an observant Jew as he does not know what to observe; he has to study in order to know how to carry out the Mitzvot. Study should not be confined to one's youth; it should continue throughout one's lifetime. Torah is like a well from which the waters of wisdom well up continually. Therefore a person has to be careful not to waste time on vain activities that may result in spiritual suicide. We have to study the Torah continually and sincerely.

REEH

(11-26) "Behold I set before you this day a blessing and a curse". In the Hebrew text the verse begins in the singular and ends in the plural, which is unusual. The reason adduced for this is that sometimes it is incumbent upon the individual to direct and guide the majority, the public, showing them the correct and proper way of life. Even when Jacob remains alone he still fights on and does not give in. We are not allowed to sit with folded arms and say everything is lost. In Judaism, if we do not go forward, then perforce we go backward, which is indicated in second verse – "The blessing is if you listen but if you will refuse to listen, then the curse may follow". As soon as you will not listen you will turn aside immediately from the road of truth, you will become heathens – "to go after other Lords which you have not known". The expression "which you have not known" has a special significance. We hear frequently from people who are not observant justifying their actions by saying that they do not understand the real reason for fulfilling the commandments. This is a lame excuse; when it comes to commit sins the same people do so without even understanding the reason and without hesitation. The real reason is that they do not want to believe. In the same context we may explain the statement by our Rabbis (Ethics 2-1): "Be heedful of a light precept as of a grave one".

The Rabbis have not warned us to "be heedful of a light sin as of a grave one". It is only when it concerns precepts that people start to weigh and measure which is light and which is grave; but when it comes to sins, everything is light and easy to transgress. Therefore the Torah has instructed our ancestors to "break down their altars and their idols", so that they may not be a stumbling block for the Israelites to entice them to transgress a commandment.

The Torah continues (12-9) – "For you are not as yet come to the rest and to the inheritance which the Lord gives you".

Rashi, commenting on the expression "come to the rest", says that it refers to Shilo where the Ark was established. That was the real place of rest and tranquillity.

The truthful place one can experience only when one is surrounded by a holy environment and atmosphere.

There we can acquire inner spiritual satisfaction and contentment. But the pursuit after empty beliefs and vain ideas is very deceiving and misleading. From afar they may look enticing and attractive, but on closer examination we discover how worthless they are and we wonder how it could have happened to us. Our regret and repentance, however, come long after our error has been committed.

This may help us to explain a statement by the Rabbis in Shabat 88. At Sinai the Lord shaped mountain as a barrel and placed it over the heads of the Israelites saying that if they would receive the Torah then everything would be well, but if they refused, that would be their grave. The expression "there" is significant, implying if you will maintain that there, when you will abandon and denounce the Torah, you will be happy and satisfied – that will be your spiritual grave.

When the Israelites received the Torah they all said together: "We shall do and listen!" The word "together" emphasizes that there has to be unity among the People of Israel. Similarly, our Rabbis interpreted the verses (4-1) – "You are the children of the Lord, you shall not cut yourself" as meaning that you shall not split your unity by establishing parties. At first glance it is difficult to understand the association, but on closer examination the following explanation may be suggested: In the same way as wounds and cuts harm the body of a person, parties, disunity and friction, weaken and destroy the nation spiritually as well as physically.

Preaching, however, is not sufficient; it has to be substantiated by practical deeds and hard facts. We have to support and help the needy and the poor, as the Torah has told us (14-22) – "You will give a tenth of thy seed". Our Rabbis add to this, saying: If you will give a tenth the Lord will enrich you. By giving charity all your possessions will multiply tenfold.

The giving of charity depends largely upon kindness and good heartedness, and there is a special reason why it was written near the injunction forbidding the cooking of milk and meat together. If a Jew eats "treif" his Jewish heart and his emotions of mercy and compassion are deadened. Consequently he stops giving charity, using various excuses and pretexts for not doing so.

You have to open your hand (15-8). The Rabbis (Bava Metzia 26) added "even a hundred times".

The following question is asked by the Rabbis: If a person wants to donate a large sum should he give it all at once or divide it in several instalments? The answer is that he should rather split it into several donations. They give this reason: It is well known that in order to develop and strengthen the body, it is necessary to have frequent exercise. The same applies to the development of kindness and of good heartedness – exercises and constant practice are required, and it is, therefore, preferable to divide the giving of charity into several instalments which will serve as a practice. If a person will give it in one time he may on occasion change his mind and be sorry for all the money he has given away. Our Rabbis, therefore, say "even a hundred times", signifying that through such practice his heart will be softened and will certainly continue and carry on the sublime and holy mitzvah of giving charity – Tzadaka.

SHOFTIM

(16-18) "Judges and officers shalt thou make for thee". The expression "for thee" may be explained as "for your benefit", meaning that if you will appoint the correct judges then you will live in peace and happiness; order and discipline will prevail in the land. Our Rabbis state (Ethics 3-2) – "Pray for the welfare of the government, since but for the fear thereof men would swallow each other alive". The proper duty of the police is to restrain and if necessary punish the criminals.

"For thee" is written in the singular. Our Rabbis say (Shabbat 119) – "Normally a person rectifies his own defects, so the Torah has emphasized "for thee" meaning, before judging others, judge first yourself, scrutinise and sit in judgment upon your deeds and actions". First cleanse yourself and then cleanse others. Judge yourself prior to judging others.

"Which the Lord is giving to your tribes". The verse continues in the singular, to emphasize that each tribe has to consider himself a partner in the establishment, welfare and security of the country. Similarly, if anything harmful or disastrous occurs in the land, before blaming others for the shortcomings, first blame oneself.

Our Rabbis stated (in Sifri) if one appoints an unsuitable judge is as he would have planted an Idol tree (Asheira).

The comparison may be explained in this manner: during the period when the Israelites worshipped idols, each one could make an idol and thereafter perform evil deeds in its name. It was not the idol who ruled and guided the person but the person was the owner of his idol. We find the same approach when people want to commit crimes, murder, steal and rob. They appoint their own judiciary and jurisprudence and in their name commit crimes, looting and killing. We have witnessed that in our times: a person "owning" the judge.

Rabon Shimon the son of Gamliel said in Ethics (2-18) – "By three things is the world preserved, by truth, by judgement and by peace".

The world is preserved by truthful judgement, which results in peace whilst false judgement results in wars, oppression and upheavals. That is obvious from King David's government (Chronicles 18-14) – "and David reigned over all Israel and he executed justice and righteousness unto all his people. And Yoav the son of Zeruiah was over the army".

David was engaged in wars during his lifetime, winning all his battles, as is stated (Samuel 11-22-38) – "I have pursued mine enemies and destroyed them, neither did I turn back till they were consumed". His soldiers loved and worshipped him, they fought like lions, sacrificing their lives in battle. The reason for their love was that they knew precisely that on returning home, David would execute justice, they would have houses to stay in and food. He prepared and provided for their material requirements abundantly, for them and their families.

On the other hand there were those leaders who neglected their soldiers, and left them in the lurch. Their promises to them were broken or remained unfulfilled, resulting in bitterness against the leaders, leading to open defiance and rebellion, the overthrow of the existing order and the death of the old leadership. The Torah therefore commands (17-18) – "and it shall be, when he sits upon the throne of his kingdom that he shall write him a copy of this law in a book, That he may prolong his day in his Kingdom". The Law of our Torah has to be constantly in his mind so that he may know properly the teachings of our faith. Promises made have to be kept so that the stability and continuity of his rule will be assured.

When the Israelites had to go to battle the following were exempted from service: a person who had planted a vineyard but had not as yet used the fruit; a person who had betrothed a wife and not taken her was equally exempted.

And then (20-7) the officers shall speak further – "What man is there that is fearful and faint-hearted, let him go and return to his house!"

Our Rabbis say that this refers to a person who is in fear of the sins which he has committed. The example is given of one who has spoken between the putting on the Tephillin on the hand and on the head, which is normally not allowed (Sota 44). This surely is difficult to understand. Assuredly this practice is not allowed by it certainly does not warrant him being told to go home!

There is a profound thought in the above statement. The ten commandments are divided into two parts, those that deal with the relationship between man and the Lord and those that cover man's dealings with man. The Tephillin on the hand symbolise the commandments which we perform with our hands like the giving of charity and helping the needy while the Tephillin on the head represent the precepts concerning man's relationship with his Maker, to believe in him unconditionally, to think rightly, and to study the Torah. However, if he made an error by saying that he believes in giving charity only and not in the importance of fulfilling other commandments, he is a partial believer; a soldier like that had to stay home. As David says (Sam. 11-22-30) – "For by thee I run upon a troop, by my G-d do I scale a wall". It was through faith and devotion to the Lord that he won the battles. So if he does not believe in the Lord he is disqualified.

"Justice, Justice you will follow" (16-20). The repetition of the word "justice" may be explained as follows: The modern revolutionaries have coined the phrase – "The aim justifies the means". Thus in the name of their aim people were murdered, oppressed or persecuted. We, however, are not allowed to use unethical means even to obtain justice, hence the repetition: Justice must be obtained through justice.

The Yalkut (Shoftim 914) states: Said Rava, "although a son has inherited a Sefer Torah, yet it is incumbent upon him to write a new Torah". The meaning of this may be given as follows: there are some of our people who are not observant Jews but boast about their parents having been religious people, observing every iota and detail of our faith. Unfortunately that is not satisfactory, each person "has to write a sefer Torah for himself". The son may not rely upon his parents, he has to write a Sefer Torah for himself.

The following will serve as an example: when hot water is decanted into a second glass the water becomes cooler, because the second glass receives the warmth from the first one so in the course of pouring it loses some of the warmth. The same applies to spiritual warmth: a son may not rely on the religious convictions of his father. He has to generate and create his own warmth and enthusiasm for our religion.

KEE-TEITZEI

The theme of the Sidra is the practice of love for people, the observance of humanitarian principles and the prohibition against shaming a friend. This has even to be observed in time of war, when soldiers are normally expected to destroy and annihilate, and when ethical and moral attitudes suffer badly. So the Torah tells us that "when you will see a woman of goodly form and you will desire her". Here the word "desire" in the text is stated "Vchushakto" which is an animal desire; you may not treat her as a slave, nor sell her for money, you may not insult her nor her family. You have to treat her humanly and lovingly. However, the soldier is reminded not to marry her hastily and regret it. After all, they belong to diverse backgrounds and may not be compatible and suited for each other. Consequently the first affection and love may quickly diminish and wane. We were commanded to respect our wife and children but not to demonstrate any favouritism or bias towards a particular child. We recall the buying by Jacob of a special shirt for Joseph which resulted in calamity for himself and his family, and their eventual exile into Egypt. Yet when parents have the problem of a stubborn and rebellious son they may not cover it up but must present him to the Beth Din for investigation and, if found guilty, has to be punished severely.

The love of parents for children may not corrupt or undermine their correct and justified judgement. If after investigation he is found guilty and sentenced to death, his body shall not remain all night upon the gallows.

(21-23) "As every person was created in the image of the Lord": even though he sinned, yet he has to be respected. The returning of a lost article to its rightful owner is an important mitzvah; one may not hide himself, but has to take it home and look after it. According to the opinion of Rav Yoseph (Bava Kama 56) the finder is even responsible if it later gets lost or stolen!

An interesting statement is made in the Talmud (Bava Metzia 32) – "If one finds two articles, one of which belongs to his enemy and the other to a friend, but he can manage to return one of them only, he has to abandon the article which belongs to his friend and instead return the article which belongs to the enemy". The reason given is that he has to break his evil inclinations. The mitzva of returning a lost article may not be fulfilled for selfish material reasons only, the finder saying to himself for example: "Today I will do my friend a favour, so he may reciprocate later". One has to do it even for an enemy, where no reward can be expected. The mitzvah has to be carried out because we were commanded to do it by the Lord and for purely humanitarian and charitable reasons. Therefore we are not allowed to spread lies and slander against anybody.

"Thou shalt not abhor an Egyptian because you were a stranger in his land" (23-8). From that we can learn how far a person has to appreciate the smallest favour done to him. Although the Egyptians oppressed us cruelly, yet we have to adopt a moral attitude towards them; we are not to hate them viciously, because we stayed in their land.

However our approach towards Amalek is different. About him it was said "blot out the remembrance of Amalek from under the heaven" (25-19). For he attacked us suddenly without any provocation and with a venomous hatred. All his intentions were to wipe us out without any excuse or pretext, all because of our belief.

The different expressions about Amalek have already been remarked upon: Exo (17-19) states – "I will utterly blot out the remembrance of Amalek" whilst the text here is "You will blot out".

The explanation is as follows: Amalek's anger and animosity against us was because of our faith, our belief in the Lord. At the time when we left Egypt we were physically weak and did not possess the courage and audacity to stand up against the mighty forces of Amalek so the Lord said that He would "blot out Amalek". After forty years of wandering in the desert during which the Israelites grew strong and gained victories, the Lord imposed the duty on them to wage war against Amalek. The Torah assured us that they would be victorious so long as unity would prevail amongst them. That is underlined in the first verse of the Sidra which is written in the singular – "when you go forth to battle and the Lord will deliver them in your hand". In unity lies strength. However, in that unity the Lord must also be included.

KEE-TAVO

(26-1) "And it will be when you will come in, in the land which the Lord gives you for an inheritance and you will possess and dwell therein, You will take of the first of all the fruit of the ground which you will bring in from your land, that the Lord gives you." The first fruit had to be given to the Priest.

The commentators have already remarked about the fact that the above verses are written in the Hebrew text in the singular. This may be explained as follows: the first mitzva commanded to them to fulfil on entering the land was "Bikurim", namely the first fruit had to be brought for the Lord. The reason for this decree is that it was incumbent upon them to give the first and best to the Lord – to demonstrate the appreciation to the Lord and to proclaim his holy name. They were also to give charity and support for the needy.

It was not necessary for a person to become affluent and then give charity. Even a poor person was commanded to give charity. He might not rely upon others to give for him, saying: "Let the rich give!" The verse was, therefore, written in the singular to admonish the individual not to shirk his duty, not to hide himself under the cover of others.

When the farmer brought his first fruit (Bikurim) it was his duty to read and narrate before the Priest the history of our people, what happened to us in Egypt, how we were enslaved, oppressed, and how the Lord redeemed us from slavery to freedom. The reason for saying that is logical. The rich person has to remember how he suffered hunger and poverty while he was poor and by keeping fresh those bad days in his memory he would possibly be encouraged to help and support the poor and the unfortunate.

The following is told about the late Gaon Rabbi Eliahau Chaim:

It was a severe winter so he went out to collect money for the poor to enable them to buy wood. He went to a certain rich person. When the rich man saw him through the window he went out in the passage to welcome the Gaon. The Rabbi was dressed in a warm overcoat; the rich man had a jacket only. The Rabbi tarried for a while in the passage which was cold, discussing an interesting topic. The host, out of respect, did not dare to interrupt the Gaon. However, when the Rabbi noticed the rich man shivering they went straight into the warm home. The latter, after giving him a fine donation, asked the Rabbi: "Why did you keep me so long in the passage? I nearly froze". To that the Rabbi replied: "I have done it purposely. If I would have come straight in to your house where you are sitting in comfort and warmth and I would have described to you the plight and misery of the unfortunate people who have no means to buy wood, it would have sounded incredible to you, but when you felt bodily the frost and the cold – you gave a generous donation." Thus the Torah told the wealthy person to remember his poverty so that he should give wholeheartedly and generously. The Mishna in Bikurim (Chap. 3-7) states that at first every farmer who brought the Bikurim (first fruit) read the portion of the law dealing with Bikurim; for the ignorant farmer somebody else read on his behalf. Later on, however, the Rabbis changed the procedure. In order not to embarrass the ignoramus it was established that a special person should be appointed to be the official reader for everyone, even for those who were able to read. In regard to this amendment, the Tosfat-Yom-Tor asked the following question: The Mishna states that the wealthy brought the fruit to the holy temple in golden baskets while the poor carried them in baskets made of reeds, so in order not to embarrass the poor, why was not it established that even the rich should bring their fruits in wooden baskets?

The question may be answered as follows: In those days an ignoramus was considered a great shame for his whole family, so in order to avoid the unnecessary insult, it was provided that a special reader should be appointed. But wealth and poverty are ordained by the Lord, as King Solomon said (Pro. 22-2): "The rich and the poor meet together. The Lord is the maker of them all". So it is definitely not an embarrassment. In our times, however, in some places values and attitudes have changed: ignorance is no longer considered a shame!

The Mishna (3 in Bikurim) states that those who live near the Holy Temple brought fresh fruit, but those whose homes were far distant brought dried fruits. That may be explained allegorically: To those who are near to Judaism, their belief is fresh and full of vitality, but as for those who are far from our faith, their Judaism consists of visiting the Shul three times a year only; their belief is dry, lifeless and mutilated.

The poor person brought his Bikurim in a reed basket constructed from a willow branch which has no taste nor smell and he placed the basket before the Lord. This signifies that if even a simple person who has no taste of our Torah or who unfortunately did not have an opportunity to study Torah, places himself before the Lord, sacrificing his personal interest on the altar of our faith, then his offering will be as acceptable as that of the most religious person.

(28-3) "Blessed you will be in the city and blessed you will be in the field". Our Rabbis comment: "The blessing is that your house should be near the synagogue". We may interpret it in this manner: Some of our brethren whom we encounter in Shul pray with fervour and warmth, exclaiming the "Shma" loudly; yet their home is not based upon religion, the food is treif, the Shabbat is desecrated. That is why it was stated that the promises and vows which you have uttered in Shul should be near to your house; they should not be contradicted in your home. The promises which you made in the synagogue must be compatible with your home life.

(2-4) "Blessed will be the fruit of your body (children) and the fruit of your land". The commentators have remarked on the fact that in the blessings the children are mentioned first and then the possessions; whilst in the curses the possessions are given preference over the children.

This may be explained thus: People who are greedy to enrich themselves invariably neglect the upbringing of their children. To them money is more important than their children. Thus at the curses, the most important aspect in their lives is mentioned first, to be cursed. Moreover that was the cause of the curses, because they did not bring up their children correctly.

NITZAVIM

(29-9) "You are standing this day, all of you, before the Lord". Rashi adds that Moses gathered them before the Lord on the day of his death to effect a mutual covenant.

The Yalkut states that the Lord made three covenants with the Israelites. (1) When they left Egypt. (2) At Mount Sinai. (3) Before his death.

The necessity for the three covenants may be explained as follows: At the time when they left Egypt the Lord promised them that they would be his nation, to be free physically and spiritually, not to tolerate slavery, humiliation and subjugation. They naturally agreed to carry it out. Unfortunately, however, no sooner had they promised it than it was broken. Immediately they rose against Moses and exclaimed – "Let us appoint a leader who will lead us back to Egypt". Moreover they expressed their longings for the garlic and onions of Egypt.

At Mount Sinai they again made a promise to believe in the Lord only and not to worship idols, yet they made a golden calf and said "This is your Lord, Israel who took you out from Egypt" – Thus Moses made another covenant before his death hoping that finally they would stand by their promise and not disappoint him. Moses indirectly reminded them about their inconsistency in the past. "You know when we dwelt in Egypt", reminding them about the covenant in Egypt – to go and worship other Lords. That was a hint about the second promise to believe in the Lord only.

(29-17) "Lest there should be among you a root that bears gall and wormwood". He referred to the spiritual shortcomings among the people. The root is the foundation of a tree, so if the root is healthy and strong then the branches and fruit will be strong and healthy. In faith and religion we also need a strong root; that is the child requires a perfect education from his youth, he has to be firmly rooted from his early youth. As the Msilat Yesharim states: "The foundation of piety and the root of religion is to be aware what is the purpose of man in life".

The root is not visible to the eye, so one has to dig down in order to examine thoroughly its real condition. About the sickness of gall and wormwood, the Even-Ezra states: "They are infectious diseases which need special precautions". Similarly, special and strict supervision is necessary over the youth who may be influenced by wicked friends. These are hidden from the eye and it is necessary to look for them.

(29-18) "That he will bless himself in the heart, saying, I shall have peace though I walk in the stubbornness of my heart".

The thoughts of a person are hidden and the hypocrite is able to mislead others as Esau deceived his father Isaac; hence the Torah has warned (29-28) – "The secret things belong to the Lord". The Lord knows the secret thoughts of people and will punish them openly for the sins which were perpetrated secretly.

As our Rabbis state (Sota 3) – "a person who commits a sin secretly, the Lord will punish him openly". (29-28) But the things that are revealed belong to us and to our children. The children will suffer because of the sins of the parents. "And you will listen to his voice". It may not be observed in a parrotlike manner, but it has to emanate rather from sincere love, and you may not say (30-12) – "Who shall go up for us to heaven and bring it to us and make us to hear it that we may do it?" This implies that there are people who say that the Torah belongs to heaven, it was originally intended for angels who have neither problems nor economic difficulties. According to the Baal-Haturim, Moses was privileged to ascend to heaven because he fulfilled the mitzva of "Meelah" (circumcision). This may be explained as follows: Meelah in our times has been almost universally accepted, even by non-Jews as a matter of health, but previously it was criticised even by the so-called enlightened Jews as a primitive custom, a relic of the wilderness. However Moses did not take notice of those who mocked and laughed at him, he followed his own conviction and religious conscience. That is invariably the criterion of a great person. He listens to the voice which comes from the depth of his heart. As the Lord said to the Prophet Isaiah (Chap. 6-9): "and he said:

Go and tell this people, Hear you indeed, but understand not. And see you indeed but perceive not", meaning that the people listen but refuse to understand, they see but are reluctant to learn, they abuse and want to undermine him. But the prophet is dauntless, he refuses to be intimidated and says: "Here am I, send me!"

(30-13) "Neither is it beyond the sea that you should say who shall go over the sea for us and bring it to us and make us to hear it". Our Rabbis compare life to the sea and each person possesses a boat, wishing and aiming to bring it safely to port. But there are dangers which he may encounter – storms and strong winds. These people use these as an excuse for not carrying out the tenets of the Torah. They claim that it is beyond their ability and physical strength "to guide their boat" and remain an observant Jew. But that is only a pretext, to avoid responsibility.

(30-14) "But the word is very near to you, in the mouth and in your heart that you may do it".

VAYELECH

(30-1) "And Moses went and spoke these words to all Israel". The commentators ask: Where did Moses go? The text is very ambiguous on that point. The Targum Yona Ben Uziel suggests: "He went to the temple to study", which may be interpreted to mean that people who are spiritually in a static position, who do not make progress in their studies and knowledge. However, if they would go to the "Temple" where they would have the opportunity to study, acquire knowledge, then they would promote themselves to higher standards and spheres of wisdom. Such a person is called "a goer", so Moses by going to the Temple went into a higher circle of knowledge.

It may also be explained according the quotation: "He went to make them aware about his impending death", and he told them he goes – namely, a person does die suddenly but goes every minute to his grave, every minute which passes does not come back, thus he said: "I am today a hundred and twenty years". His whole 120 years seemed to him like a day; life is like a dream. So the expression "Moses went" means he was departing from the world.

"I cannot no more go out and come in" (31-2). Rashi comments that it refers to his spiritual ability – "I am not able to discuss the wise words of the Torah, I am powerless to come in on a Torah discussion". Physically Moses was healthy and vigorous, he ascended the mountain Nevo; but spiritually he was dying, he could not understand the wise words of Torah; for him life was of no avail.

The Lord "created man in his image". Rashi's comment is: The image of the Lord is to understand and be wise, so it follows that when a person lacks understanding of the holy words of Torah, he is considered as if the image of the Lord had disappeared from him. Moses also admitted – "I can no more go out" – and he handed over the leadership to Yehoshua in the presence of the people. He was young and was chosen by the Lord to lead the people (31-9): "And Moses wrote this law and delivered it to the Priests, the sons of Levi that bore the Ark of the covenant of the Lord".

Moses was afraid that perhaps after his death the people might start to shorten and reform the Torah, so he handed over the Torah to the Priests who would be responsible for its safety and authenticity. Because of that they will be assured of a great and bright future. The Talmud (Sanhedrin 90) narrates that the Romans asked the great Rabbi Yoshua, the son of Chanania: "Where is it mentioned in the Bible about the resurrection of the dead?" To which he replied: "It is indicated in (31-6) – "And this people will rise up". That may be explained in the light of historical events. At that time the Hebrews were oppressed and crushed by the Romans, whose final aim was to annihilate us. They maintained that their goal had already been attained. There was no hope for our return to Israel. Physically and spiritually we were subdued and downtrodden. But the Rabbi contradicted him. "The people will rise again", he said. They may sin, deviate from the correct path, yet they will return to their own home land.

That is the resurrection of the dead. From their graves they will proceed to nationhood and independence.

The Talmud (in Chulin) asks where in the Torah is the miracle of Esther mentioned. The answer is given (31-18): "And I will surely hide my face in that day for all the evil which they shall have wrought". In Hebrew the word for hide is "astir"; the name Ester is also derived from the same root, to hide. But what is the association with the context? That may be explained as follows: According to our tradition a great miracle has occurred to us on Purim. We were saved from Haman who schemed to destroy us.

However there are some who wish to explain it in a natural manner. The King of Persia fell in love with Ester, subsequently she became a queen and when her people were threatened she helped them. But our Rabbis have stated that Ester was neither beautiful nor young. The King was surrounded by many charming, young and pretty girls, yet he chose Ester, because it was ordained by the Lord that she would save her people. It was a hidden miracle. As King Solomon says in Song of Songs (2-9): "He stands behind our wall, he looks in through the windows, he peers through the lattice".

When two people meet face to face then they see each other but if one is watching through the lattice, then the person who is in the house can see his friend but not otherwise. In the bygone days the miracles were open, then we also could see the presence of the Lord. Now we are experiencing hidden miracles so the Lord does see us but we are not able to perceive the presence of the Lord. That was the miracle of Ester, a hidden miracle. The very fact that we have survived and returned to Israel is in itself a hidden miracle indeed. As it was said in our day – "one has to be a realist in order to believe in miracles".

HAAZEENU

(32-1) "Give ear you heavens and I will speak". Why at that stage did Moses address himself to the heavens? The above Sidra contains the farewell words of Moses, harsh, critical, admonishing. By nature people are not enthusiastic to listen to critical sermons, they prefer compliments and praise. Moses was afraid that the people might desert him, so he directed his words towards heaven.

(2) "My doctrine shall drip as the rain". The Yalkut relates: When Moses went up to heaven the angels wanted to kill him so he told them words of Torah and was consequently saved. He compared the Torah to rain drops.

The question is obvious: Why did not Moses tell them that story before now? There is a feasible reason for that. Moses wanted to criticise them. Normally there is a dissatisfied reaction to criticism – people react bitterly by saying – "who are you to criticise us? On what authority are you basing it? First cleanse yourself before embarking on running down others!" Hence Moses told them that he had endangered his life for the Torah, therefore he had the moral right to reprimand and reprove them. He continues (3) – "For I will proclaim the name of the Lord, ascribe your greatness on our G-d".

He exclaims: "Give honour to the creator and listen to my words".

(4) "The Rock, his work is perfect". The Lord is like a rock who protects and shields us; yet he is unlike the rock which sometimes harms and bruises, he is perfect. As for punishment, we have to

accept the blame. (5) "Is corruption His? No, His children are the blemish, a generation crooked and perverse". (6) "A foolish people and unwise".

The Targum Onkelos comments: "A nation which received the Torah". Actually that comment does not correspond to the text. If they received the Torah why are they called foolish?

This may be explained as follows: If a person has been brought up in an environment of ignorance and was not afforded an opportunity to study he has a legitimate excuse for his shortcomings; however, if a person has been surrounded by pure minded, intellectual and learned people and yet grew up wild, unmannered and uncouth, that person has no excuse and pretext for his boorishness and stupidity. That was the comment of the Targum: "You who have received the Torah and yet you persist in your foolishness, you are indeed an unwise people!"

(32-15) You received the Torah and kicked. In that verse the people of Israel are named "Yeshurun" which is derived from the Hebrew word "Yosher" – "equity and honesty". We who received the Torah, are expected to act honestly and sincerely in our dealings and endeavours to appreciate the Lord and yet we kicked. If, therefore, a nation does not possess a sense of appreciation it will sink low morally and ethically. He continues (32-21): "They have roused me to jealousy with their vanities. They have provoked me with their vanities".

In our community we encounter Jews who abuse and mock at fundamentals of our religion and holiness and yet believe in all kinds of superstitions and false beliefs. To quote one example about which I had been told. A Jewish mother organised a birthday party for her child on Shabbat. As customary, the required number of candles were lit on Shabbat, then the child was told to blow them out. As it happened he did not blow them out in one go. Immediately the mother started to worry saying that it was a bad sign. She did not worry about the desecration of Shabbat but was upset and downhearted because of a stupid and silly superstitious custom. This was exactly what Moses had reprimanded them about. Judaism, which is logical and sensible, you have rejected, but you believe in foulness, in hanging a horseshoe, number 13, etc. Moses concludes his advice (32-43): "Sing aloud O ye nations of his people. For he does avenge the blood of his servants".

We may interpret this as follows: In our long Galut we have been oppressed and killed. But who could ever have imagined the cruelty and bestiality of the Nazis? Who could have dreamed that human beings should sink so low, that so-called civilised people should turn into beasts? When our brethren were thrown in the burning furnaces they stood around with their orchestras playing, dancing and singing amicably and joyfully. So Moses has told us if and when our enemies will reach such a low ebb of humanity then the Lord will avenge our innocent blood, then we shall return to our land!

V'ZOT – HABRACHA

The Yalkut states: "Beelam the wicked was jealous at the blessings which the people of Israel received". Then Moses came; he loved them and was overjoyed with their blessings. "Let him bless them". What was his blessing? – "May it be the will of the Lord that the presence of the Lord may dwell in all your deeds". This is the Sedra of V'zot Habracha (this is the blessing). Beelam was a venomous enemy of our people even in his blessings; his intentions were that by his blessings the Israelites would be punished.

This may be illustrated by the following example. When a person who is accused of theft appears before a judge and tries to gain his acquittal by justifying his action, saying that his despicable behaviour was due to the fact that his father was also a thief, so that the environment and evil upbringing were responsible for his moral degradation. That excuse may be accepted by the judge and his sentence may be lenient. But if his father were a Rabbi then naturally the sentence will be more severe. That was the intention of Beelam when he exclaimed: "How goodly are your tents Jacob" – meaning look at your background, examine the rock from which you have been hewn; your sin is greater, consequently the sentence will be more severe.

Moses, however, said: "May the presence of the Lord rest in your deeds"; that is: may the Lord not examine and scrutinise your past, but look at the present only. Let Him look at the difficult conditions in which you find yourselves.

(33-1) "Moses the Man of G-d". The Yalkut says that when Moses went up to receive the Torah, he was called "a man" only, but when he descended to the earth he was called "Man of G-d". The following interpretation may be given to this statement: We all know that the Torah was not given for angels, thus if Moses would have been a person of G-d, that is an angel, when he was given the Torah, then we would have had an excuse for our sins. We could then argue, saying that the Torah was not meant for us who are ordinary human beings, but was rather intended for Moses who was like an angel. His was a high spiritual status, therefore he was able to fulfil the mitzvot. But we are unfortunately ignorant and backward in comparison to Moses, therefore it states that Moses while he was afflicted with the usual faults and weaknesses, yet he received the Torah to show that even an ordinary person can observe the Torah. But when he went down he was a man of G-d, which shows the greatness of our Torah. Through study and observance an ordinary person is able to attain great spiritual heights.

Around the Tents of Torah

"The Lord came from Sinai". The Yalkut says that when the Lord appeared to give the Torah to the people of Israel he did not appear from one side only, but appeared from the four corners of the world. That comes to signify that it is impossible for a Jew to be assimilated and to run away from the Lord and Judaism because wherever he will go there is no escape from the Lord. The Lord has his ways and means of reminding him that he is a Jew, someone will sooner or later remind him of his ancestry.

(34-6) "And he was buried (Moses) in the valley in the land of Moab, and no man knew of his sepulchre until this day". The Yalkut states: "Ramei, the son of Hama, said: 'Even Moses himself does not know his grave'," which may be explained. Moses is called the servant of the Lord even after his death (Joshua 1-1). Because so long as we continue the study of the Torah Moses remains alive – he is dead physically but not spiritually. However, that depends on us, his spiritual children. If we visit the synagogues (Yeshivot) regularly and conscientiously and fulfil the commandments, then his grave is non-existent, he remains active and very much alive. As the Talmud states: "Rava says: 'Actually they cannot say any more as they are already dead, but spiritually as it were they are still standing in front of us and are teaching us, provided that we still continue to study their teachings'". Likewise our Rabbis state: "When we repeat a statement or an opinion of a dead person his lips are moving in the grave". This is explained as above: If we still remember the teachings of that particular deceased person then he is still alive, his lips are still moving but if we abandon his teachings then he is spiritually dead. Thus, that is what Rabbi Ramei said that Moses does not know his spiritual demise; that does not depend upon him, it is rather connected with us, with the coming generations. If we shall continue to devote ourselves to the teachings of Moses then he will remain alive. It is our imperative duty to do so. Said Rabbi Simloee: the

Torah ends on a note of charity and begins on the same note, charity. In the end it states that the Lord buried Moses, which is charity to the dead and begins with charity (Gen. 3-21) – "and the Lord made for Adam and for his wife garments of skins and clothed them, which is also charity". Charity and kindness to the poor is one of the fundamental principles of our belief. There is charity to the dead like attending the dead to the grave (Mishna Peah) which is not a difficult Mitzva to carry out. But the Torah has many a time repeated to us that the most important mitzva for us to carry out is the charity and kindness to the living, to prevent them from dying. Life is more important than death. We are even allowed to desecrate the Shabbat to preserve life.

King David (Psalms 115-17) has summed it up: "The dead praise not the Lord, neither any that go down in silence, but we will bless the Lord from this time forth and for ever more".

The Torah ends with the letter "Lamed", which stands for Study, signifying that even on finishing the Torah we still have to continue to study as the Torah has neither a beginning nor an end. The Gaon has likewise said: "The Torah starts with the letter 'Beit' and not with the 'Aleph' which is the first letter in the alphabet, to impress upon us that we have not even started to study the alphabet".